ESRI

The Economic and Social Research Institute

The Economic and Social Research Institute (ESRI) is a non-profit organisation which was founded in 1960 as The Economic Research Institute. The Institute is a private company, limited by guarantee, and enjoys full academic independence. It is governed by a Council consisting of 32 members who are representative of business, trade unions, government departments, state agencies, universities and other research institutes.

DO SCHOOLS DIFFER?

Academic and Personal Development among Pupils in the Second-Level Sector

Emer Smyth

Oak Tree Press

Dublin

in association with
The Economic and Social Research Institute

Oak Tree Press
Merrion Building
Lower Merrion Street
Dublin 2, Ireland
http://www.oaktreepress.com

A catalogue record of this book is
available from the British Library.

ISBN 1-86076-118-6

This study forms part of The Economic and Social Research Institute's
General Research Series, in which it is Paper No. 173. It has been
subject to the normal internal and external refereeing procedures
employed for that series and accepted for publication by the Institute,
which is not responsible for either the content or
the views expressed therein.

Printed in Ireland by Colour Books Ltd.

CONTENTS

LIST OF TABLES

LIST OF FIGURES

ACKNOWLEDGEMENTS

This study was funded by the Department of Education and Science. In particular, I am grateful to Gearóid Ó Conluain, Carl Ó Dálaigh and Denis Healy for their support for the project.

This research would not have been possible without the earlier work on coeducation carried out with my colleagues: Damian Hannan, John McCullagh, Richard O'Leary and Dorren McMahon. Damian continued to provide support during the current project. I wish to reiterate my thanks to the school principals, staff and pupils who took part in the initial survey of second-level schools. I am particularly grateful to all of the staff who very generously gave of their time during the detailed case-studies of schools.

Selina McCoy contributed greatly to the school case-studies through her skilful interviewing and incisive comments on earlier drafts of the material. Within the ESRI, I would also like thank Breda McCabe, Pat Hopkins and Deirdre Whitaker for helping to bring the project to this stage.

The book owes much to the comments and suggestions of two internal ESRI referees, Chris Whelan and Denis Conniffe, along with those of an anonymous external referee. I am also grateful to Peter Daly, Queen's University Belfast, and Richard Breen, European University Institute, for extremely helpful comments on earlier drafts of the study.

Any remaining errors or omissions are the sole responsibility of the author.

ABOUT THE AUTHOR

Dr Emer Smyth is a Research Officer at the Economic and Social Research Institute. She holds a doctorate in Sociology from University College Dublin. Her areas of interest include education, school to work transitions, and women's employment. She has worked on a large-scale national study of the impact of coeducation on pupil outcomes, published as *Coeducation and Gender Equality*, and is currently involved in a comparative study of labour market transitions among young people in several European countries.

Chapter 1

INTRODUCTION

International research has highlighted the fact that "school matters" (Mortimore *et al.*, 1988), that is, that school organisation and process have an impact on pupil achievement and development which is independent of between-school differences in pupil intake. In the Irish context, the *Coeducation and Gender Equality* study (Hannan, Smyth *et al.*, 1996) has indicated that schools vary significantly in the academic performance and personal/social development of their pupils, and that a school effect persists even when pupil composition is taken into account.

In recent years, the implications of school effects research for policy relating to school effectiveness and school improvement have come increasingly to the fore internationally. The introduction of a system for school assessment has proved particularly controversial in Britain. The publication of "league tables" ranking schools in terms of their average exam grades has been criticised for ignoring between-school differences in pupil intake and for increasing polarisation between schools, as certain groups of parents actively select "higher-performing" schools. The development of these "performance indicators" has been accompanied by the introduction of a national programme of school inspection which has proved no less controversial (Earley *et al.*, 1996; Ouston *et al.*, 1996). While there has been much less debate about such issues in the Irish context, a concern with school improvement issues was also apparent in the *White Paper on Education*, which stressed the need for a complementary policy of whole school inspection and self-auditing on the part of schools. More recently, the Department of Education has introduced a pilot project on whole-school evaluation as a basis for school-based development and planning.

The main aim of this study is to identify the key schooling processes associated with enhanced academic and development outcomes among pupils. International research has highlighted a number of factors which contribute to school effectiveness in relation to different pupil outcomes and groups of pupils. However, there are reasons for interpreting these findings with caution when examining the Irish situation. First, cross-national research indicates that the factors influencing pupil performance may vary across educational systems (Scheerens and Bosker, 1997). Therefore, it cannot be assumed that international findings are applicable in the Irish context. Second, many studies specify broad factors, such as "school ethos", without providing specific guidelines on how these factors can be assessed or measured. Third, studies have tended to view school effectiveness in terms of pupil achievement alone, rather than taking account of the impact of schools on a range of pupil outcomes. This study arose from a concern by the Department of Education to inform policy development with information on the specific nature of second-level schools in Ireland.

Definitions of school effectiveness are far from uncontroversial:

> Effectiveness is not a neutral term. Defining the effective-
> ness of a particular school always requires choices among
> competing values. (Firestone, 1991, p.2)

While the primary focus of research has been on assessing school effects on educational development, defining criteria for such development is far from clear-cut. Should the concern be with performance in national exams or do standardised test scores represent a more adequate measure? Should the measure(s) reflect aggregate performance or achievement in particular subjects (or subject areas)? It is also unclear whether other pupil outcomes reflecting aspects of pupil personal/social development should be considered in conjunction with academic progress. The task of assessing school effectiveness is particularly difficult in the context of the complex and often conflicting set of goals facing management and staff in second-level schools.

For the purposes of this study, a multidimensional view of effectiveness is adopted; a school may be seen as "effective" in relation to academic performance, personal/social development, pupil absenteeism and/or pupil retention. The multidimensional nature of the study allows us to examine whether schools are effective across a range of aspects, promoting educational attainment but also enhancing social development among pupils, for instance; or whether some schools optimise exam performance but at the expense of higher drop-out rates among low ability pupils or high stress levels among pupils (see Chapter 9). The concern is with assessing the influence of school organisation and process on the "average" pupil but also on particular groups of pupils, in particular, those of different ability levels (see Chapter 8). The focus in this study is not on "ranking" individual schools in terms of their effectiveness but on identifying characteristics which are associated with enhanced pupil outcomes. It is hoped that these characteristics can be used as a basis for developing models of good practice for all second-level schools. However, it must be recognised that the process of school improvement is complex and may involve more than the simple transfer of models of good organisational practice from more effective to less effective schools (see Reynolds, 1995).

1.1 IMPORTANCE OF SCHOOL EFFECTS

Earlier research on school effects (Coleman *et al.*, 1966; Jencks *et al.*, 1972) reached rather pessimistic conclusions about the potential effects of school organisation and process on pupil outcomes. Researchers argued that family background and prior ability represent the main influences on academic performance, and that there are no substantive differences between schools in pupil performance once these factors have been taken into account. More recent studies have challenged these claims arguing that schools can make a substantive impact on their pupils and that the school attributes that make a difference are amenable to intervention (see, for example, Rutter *et al.*, 1979; Mortimore *et al.*, 1988; Teddlie and Stringfield, 1993). Often the disagreement is not about the overall size of school effects but about the interpretation of the significance of these effects. Many researchers agree that a relatively "low" proportion of variation in pupil outcomes is associated with schools (see Preece, 1989; Gray *et al.*, 1990). A meta-analysis of a number of international studies across the primary and secondary sectors indicates that, on average, schools account for 19 per cent of overall achievement differences among pupils, a figure which is reduced to 8 per cent when adjustment is made for pupil differences (Scheerens and Bosker, 1997). Consequently, the debate focuses on whether school effects, while relatively small in comparison with variation among pupils in terms of social background, prior ability and so on, may be significant in educational terms (Sammons, Hillman, Mortimore, 1995).

Discussion about school effects has become more prominent over the 1980s and 1990s for two reasons. First, the development of more sophisticated statistical techniques (such as multi-level modelling) has facilitated more precise estimates of the effects of school characteristics over and above differences in pupil intake. These studies have found that, while a substantial degree of the variation between schools in pupil performance can be explained by differences in the intake of pupils to those schools, substantive differences are apparent between schools even when these differences are taken into account (Smith and Tomlinson, 1989; Sammons, Hillman, Mortimore, 1995; Thomas and Mortimore, 1996).

Second, recent educational policy in Britain has emphasised the assessment of schools in terms of their examination results. The value of publishing such "league tables" of schools has been challenged by academic researchers on a number of grounds (Woodhouse and Goldstein, 1988).

1.   Such rankings do not take into account differences in pupil intake between schools; thus, a "good" performance may merely reflect a selective intake in terms of prior pupil ability and social class. It is argued that it is more appropriate to view school effectiveness in terms of the "value added" by the school, that is, the overall contribution a school makes to the development of each of its pupils (Birnbaum, 1994; Sammons *et al.*, 1994).

2.   The ranking of schools may vary over time and between subject areas or departments (see below). Academic performance in a particular school may vary from year to year. In addition, a school may be particularly "effective" in English but "ineffective" in relation to Mathematics.

3.   All such rankings are subject to measurement error (Woodhouse and Goldstein, 1996). Adjusted rankings often use data from surveys of samples of pupils to derive the "adjustment" criteria; consequently, characteristics, such as social class, may be imprecisely measured and are subject to sample variation.

4.   It has been found that fine distinctions and detailed rank orderings are statistically invalid even when adjustments have been made for pupil intake (Goldstein *et al.*, 1993; Kendall, 1995; Goldstein and Spiegelhalter, 1996). These

analyses can enable us to make broad-brush statements about the characteristics associated with effectiveness but finely ordered rankings of schools must be regarded as inappropriate (Gray, 1995).

1.2 DEFINING SCHOOL EFFECTIVENESS

Most of the research on school effects has focused solely on academic outcomes among pupils. In standardised educational systems, such as England and Scotland, academic outcomes tend to be measured in terms of examination results (see, for example, Goldstein *et al.*, 1993). In other systems, such as the United States, outcomes are measured in terms of standardised ability test scores (see, for example, Teddlie and Stringfield, 1993). When pupil performance is the outcome of interest, an effective school can be defined as one in which pupils progress further academically than might be predicted on the basis of the attainment of its intake (Sammons *et al.*, 1994).

In comparison, studies which focus on both academic and non-academic outcomes among pupils are comparatively rare. Some studies have considered pupil behaviour (Rutter *et al.*, 1979; Mortimore *et al.*, 1988) and/or personal/social development (such as academic self-image, locus of control) among pupils (see Brookover *et al.*, 1979; Bryk *et al.*, 1993). However, findings have differed concerning the relationship between academic and non-academic outcomes. Mortimore's study indicated no discernible relationship between school effects in relation to cognitive and non-cognitive outcomes (see also Brookover *et al.*, 1979), while Rutter's study indicated that schools which did better in terms of exam success also did better in terms of pupil behaviour and delinquency. More recently, researchers have stressed the need to study a broad range of educational and developmental outcomes of the schooling process (Knuver and Brandsma, 1989; Creemers and Scheerens, 1994; Gray, 1995).

1.3 FACTORS INFLUENCING SCHOOL EFFECTIVENESS

Research on school effects indicates a number of areas of agreement on the factors influencing pupil outcomes. Due to the focus of previous research on cognitive outcomes, many of these factors relate to effectiveness in academic rather than broader developmental terms.

(i) School Context

A number of studies have found that the social context of the school can have an effect on pupil outcomes, over and above the social background of the individual pupil. Studies of schools in England, Scotland and the US have indicated that pupils tend to do worse academically in schools with a high concentration of pupils from working-class and/or disadvantaged backgrounds (Bryk and Raudenbush, 1988; Lee and Bryk, 1989; Paterson, 1991; Croxford and Cowie, 1996). It has also been found that the social mix of the school has a greater impact on pupils from disadvantaged backgrounds than on other pupils (Croxford and Robertson, 1996). In addition, one American study has indicated that the correlates of school effectiveness can vary according to the social context of the school (Teddlie and Stringfield, 1993). However, other studies have found relatively weak evidence of compositional effects (Gray *et al.*, 1990; Lee and Smith, 1995) and have argued that, where detailed pupil intake data are available, school context factors are not significant in predicting pupil outcomes (Thomas and Mortimore, 1996).

The "academic balance" within the school has been found to have a significant impact, with pupils performing better in schools where there are higher overall levels of pupil ability (Rutter *et al.*, 1979; Willms, 1985). However, research on comprehensive schools in Britain has indicated no contextual effects from the ability or ethnic mix within the school (Smith and Tomlinson, 1989).

(ii) School Management and Staffing

A number of American studies have focused on the impact of "school quality" (as measured by the pupil-teacher ratio) on pupil performance. While some studies have indicated an association between higher pupil-teacher ratios and lower pupil performance in standardised ability tests (see, for example, Loeb and Bound, 1996), much of the research has been inconclusive (Hanushek, 1986). In the British context, one study has indicated that higher pupil-teacher ratios are associated with higher pupil drop-out (Dustmann *et al.*, 1996), although a study using data on more recent cohorts of school leavers has indicated no such effect (Cheng, 1995). In general, the relationship between pupil-teacher ratios and the size of the class within which learning takes place is likely to be mediated by management decisions concerning allocation of staff and curricular provision within the school.

Findings regarding the importance of school management styles in pupil outcomes have been more consistent. Research has indicated that the school principal plays a crucial role and that schools are effective where there is firm and purposeful leadership (Rutter *et al.*, 1979; Mortimore *et al.*, 1988). A more participative style, involving staff in decision-making processes and developing shared goals among staff, is associated with greater effectiveness (Purkey and Smith, 1983; Lee and Smith, 1995; National Commission on Education, 1996; Scheerens and Bosker, 1997; Hallinger and Heck, 1998). An emphasis on school-based staff development plays a crucial role in school improvement (Purkey and Smith, 1983; Sammons, Hillman, Mortimore, 1995); in particular, the way in which new teachers are integrated into the school through formal or informal induction programmes plays a key role in fostering collegiality and shared educational goals (Teddlie and Stringfield, 1993). Low staff turnover has been found to be associated with more positive pupil outcomes (Purkey and Smith, 1983) while high turnover is associated with higher pupil truancy (Casey and Smith, 1995) and drop-out (Cheng, 1995).

(iii) School Organisation and Class Allocation

The use of streaming/tracking techniques has been associated with a boost in performance for those in top classes and underperformance among those in bottom classes (Sorenson and Hallinan, 1984; Gamoran and Nystrand, 1994). However, American studies indicate no significant difference between streamed and unstreamed schools in average performance levels across all pupils (Gamoran and Nystrand, 1994). In the Irish context, streaming has been associated with increased variance within the school in pupil performance and with higher drop-out rates among pupils (Hannan, Boyle, 1987).

(iv) School Climate

Several aspects of school climate have been found to have a significant impact on school effectiveness. First, the disciplinary climate of the school can enhance pupil outcomes; pupils tend to do better in schools which have a clear, consistent but fair set of rules and policies and an orderly atmosphere within the school (Madaus *et al.*, 1975; Brookover *et al.*, 1979; Rutter *et al.*, 1979; Coleman *et al.*, 1982; Mortimore *et al.*, 1988; Lee, Bryk and Smith, 1993; Scheerens and Bosker, 1997). Conversely, pupil drop-out rates tend to be higher in schools with discipline problems (Bryk and Thum, 1989).

Second, the quality of interaction and amount of feedback between teachers and pupils is strongly associated with effectiveness. Pupils tend to do better in schools where they are given positive reinforcement concerning their progress through, for example, regular setting and monitoring of homework (Brookover *et al.*, 1979; Rutter *et al.*, 1979; Mortimore *et al.*, 1988). Conversely, pupils tend to do worse in schools where they experience negative interaction ("blame") from teachers (Smith and Tomlinson, 1989).

Third, the degree of academic emphasis in a school is associated with enhanced pupil performance. Pupils tend to do better in schools where management and teachers hold high expectations for them and where their peers have a strong commitment to study (Madaus *et al.*, 1975; Bryk and Raudenbush, 1988; Teddlie and Stringfield, 1993; Sammons *et al.*, 1995; Lee and Smith, 1995). A strong academic emphasis is also associated with lower levels of pupil drop-out and truancy (Rutter *et al.*, 1979; Bryk and Thum, 1989; Leithwood *et al.*, 1989).

Fourth, pupil and parental involvement in the school have been found to be associated with effectiveness, particularly for schools in disadvantaged areas (National Commission on Education, 1996). Pupils tend to do better in schools where they are involved in positions of responsibility (Rutter *et al.*, 1979) and in out-of-school activities with staff (Smith and Tomlinson, 1989; Lee, Bryk and Smith, 1993). Parental participation in the school is associated with higher performance (Wilson and Corcoran, 1988; Lee, Bryk and Smith, 1993; Sui-Chu and Willms, 1996) and lower pupil absenteeism (Mortimore *et al.*, 1988), although informal involvement may actually be more significant than formal involvement (Mortimore *et al.*, 1988).

(v) School Effectiveness and Teacher Effectiveness

There has been much debate about whether the concern should be with school effectiveness or teacher effectiveness (see, for example, Rowe and Hill, 1994; Creemers and Reezigt, 1996). School effectiveness is clearly dependent upon effective classroom teaching; in particular, the maximisation of effective learning time (Brookover *et al.*, 1979; Mortimore *et al.*, 1988; Scheerens, 1992) and the structuring of lessons (Brophy and Good, 1986; Scheerens, 1992; Scheerens and Bosker, 1997) have been found to be associated with higher pupil performance. However, research is less consistent about the effects of teachers' personal characteristics on classroom effectiveness; cross-national research indicates no significant relationship between teacher training and reading performance among nine year olds (Scheerens and Bosker, 1997).

It is more straightforward to assess the impact of teacher effectiveness in primary schools or in particular subject areas (where pupils are likely to have only one teacher per year). However, in second-level schools pupils are likely to be exposed to a number of different teachers over the period of their schooling. In addition, teacher effectiveness is likely to be influenced by organisational and curricular arrangements at school level (Sammons *et al.*, 1997). Consequently, the importance of whole-school effectiveness for facilitating effective teaching is particularly important in second-level schools which face complex organisational goals.

1.4 DIFFERENTIAL EFFECTIVENESS

Initial research on school organisation and process focused on the effects of schools on the "average" pupil. However, more recently attention has turned to the possibility that schools may be differentially effective for different groups of pupils. Evidence from second-level schools in Britain indicates that schools appear to be differentially effective for different ability pupils, that is, some schools are more effective for high ability pupils while others are more effective for low ability pupils (Nuttall *et al.*, 1989; Goldstein *et al.*, 1993; Thomas and Mortimore, 1996; Thomas *et al.*, 1997). However, researchers have differed in the variation found for different ability groups. Some have found that schools differ more in the results they achieve with higher ability pupils (Goldstein *et al.*, 1993; Smith and Tomlinson, 1989) while others have found that schools matter more for lower ability pupils (Nuttall *et al.*, 1989; Sammons *et al.*, 1993). Other research using broadly comparable data has indicated little substantive evidence for differential effectiveness (Gray *et al.*, 1990), although this may reflect differences in the type of information used on prior ability (Jesson and Gray, 1991). While much of the research has focused on differential effectiveness by ability group, other studies have indicated that schools may be differentially effective for different social class, ethnic or gender groups (Smith and Tomlinson, 1989; Nuttall *et al.*, 1989; Sammons *et al.*, 1997).

1.5 STABILITY OF SCHOOL EFFECTS

Stability of school effects can be considered in the following ways:

1.   Stability of school effectiveness over time;

2.   Stability across school years (or grades) within the school;

3.   Stability across subject areas;

4.   Stability across pupil outcomes.

Research has indicated a good deal of stability in schools' effectiveness in overall academic performance from year to year, with little movement evident over a three year period (Gray *et al.*, 1995; Sammons *et al.*, 1997). Other research has indicated some variation over time in school effects (Nuttall *et al.*, 1989) and has stressed the importance of viewing schools as dynamic organisations (Slater and Teddlie, 1992). Variation over time tends to be lower for overall performance than for individual subjects (Sammons *et al.*, 1997). Greater differences have been found between year groups of pupils than between groups of pupils over time (Mandeville and Anderson, 1987; Scheerens, 1992). However, such differences may not reflect "instability" in school effects since schools may allocate resources and teachers differently to the different year groups and/or may use different organisational arrangements (such as streaming) for different groups.

Research has indicated that schools are rarely consistently effective in different subject areas. At school level, little relationship has been found between effectiveness in English and Maths, for example, (Goldstein *et al.*, 1993; Thomas and Mortimore, 1996) and substantial differences exist within some schools in terms of departmental effectiveness over a three year period (Sammons *et al.*, 1997). Little information is available on whether schools are consistently effective for different pupil outcomes and there is little consensus on the relationship between effects on academic and non-academic outcomes (see above).

1.6 CONCLUSIONS

Research on school effectiveness has indicated a number of factors, including disciplinary climate, academic emphasis, and pupil-teacher interaction, which are consistently associated with enhanced pupil outcomes. Other research has cautioned for the need to take account of potential differential effectiveness within schools and for potential instability over time in school effectiveness.

This study will test whether the factors identified in the international literature have an impact on pupil outcomes in second-level schools in Ireland. It will also assess whether schools are differentially effective for different groups of pupils. In contrast to many previous studies, a multi-dimensional view of school effectiveness is adopted, focusing not only on academic outcomes but also on absenteeism and drop-out and on aspects of personal/social development among pupils.

The methods used in the study are outlined in the following chapter. Chapter 3 describes second-level schools in Ireland in terms of key aspects of school organisation and process. Chapters 4 and 5 assess the impact of schooling factors on Junior and Leaving Certificate exam performance, respectively. Chapter 6 examines the effects of schools on absenteeism and drop-out rates among Junior Cert pupils. Chapter 7 assesses the influence of schooling factors on personal/social development and stress levels among second-level pupils. Chapter 8 explores whether schools are equally effective for different groups of pupils. Chapter 9 assesses whether schools are consistently effective over a range of pupil outcomes, both academic and non-academic. Chapter 10 explores the existence of "outlier" schools, those which are significantly different from the average, while Chapter 11 presents detailed findings on school organisation and process in a number of these outlier schools. The conclusions of the study and the implications for policy development are presented in Chapter 12.

Chapter 2

RESEARCH METHODS

This chapter outlines the research methods adopted in the study. This study uses the data base developed for the *Coeducation and Gender Equality* study, which provides a particularly rich source of information on the characteristics of 116 second-level schools and over 10,000 pupils at Junior and Leaving Certificate levels. The sample is nationally representative and allows us to generalise to the population of second-level schools and pupils in Ireland. Four main data sources were used in the study:

1. Interviews with school principals and guidance counsellors from 116 schools across the country.

2. Questionnaires administered to Junior and Leaving Certificate pupils within these schools.

3. Ability tests administered to Junior Certificate pupils.

4. Examination data collected on the Junior and Leaving Certificate pupils in the sample, along with examination data for the sampled schools in 1996.

These data sources form the basis for the first phase of the study which focuses on assessing the impact of school characteristics on a range of pupil outcomes. The second phase of this study involves detailed case-studies of six schools in order to identify in detail the complex of school organisation and process factors characteristic of more effective and less effective schools.

2.1 SAMPLE

The sample of schools was drawn using stratified random sampling with schools selected to be representative of the national distribution of schools in terms of school sector, gender composition, school size and location. Four schools were dropped from the original sample: three had changed over to Post-Leaving Certificate colleges, while the other had just been amalgamated with two other schools. Six schools refused to co-operate with the study in spite of many efforts to secure their participation. A double sample was drawn in the community/comprehensive sector to ensure sufficient numbers of "green-field" and amalgamated schools for analysis. In other respects, the sampled schools closely match the national distribution of schools. Where necessary, schools are weighted to reflect the national population.

The years selected for study were the Junior Certificate (JC) and Leaving Certificate (LC) exam years. Classes were sampled within schools, taking roughly half the total number of classes from the relevant years in each selected school. "Classes" were defined for the purposes of the study as the "permanent" (or "base") class to which students were assigned for school organisa-tion purposes and in which they took a number of subjects or class periods together as a group. In most schools such a definition was unproblematic, although in some schools this definition did not conform with the Departmental roll class. There were a small number of schools, however, which did not have any base classes in this sense; having individual subject classes only, with a con-siderable degree of movement between subjects and levels. In these cases we sampled those subject classes which, in the princi-pal's view, corresponded most closely to the ability mix of the year. Specific sampling rules for classes took account of the use of streaming, banding or mixed ability teaching, as well as of the number of classes within the relevant years (for further details of the sampling procedure, see Hannan, Smyth *et al.*, 1996).

2.2 FIELDWORK

Interviews with school principals and guidance counsellors collected detailed information on school organisation and process including:

- the nature and packaging of the curriculum provided;

- the degree and timing of subject choice;

- the level of staffing within the school;

- systems for allocating pupils to base classes;

- the disciplinary climate within the school;

- formal involvement of parents in the school;

- formal involvement of pupils in the school;

- the level of drop-out from school over the junior and senior cycles;

- the provision of formal pastoral care programmes within the school.

Interviews with school principals and guidance counsellors were conducted by members of the ESRI interview team over the period December 1993 to March 1994.

In total, 5,961 Junior Cert pupils and 4,813 Leaving Cert pupils completed the administered questionnaires. Almost all of the fieldwork was completed by mid-March 1994. The pupil questionnaires covered such topics as:

- subjects and levels taken by the pupil;

- social background of the pupil;

- attitudes to certain subject areas, such as Maths and Science;

- degree of satisfaction with school;

- perceptions of school climate;

- perceptions of interaction with teachers;

- perceptions of teacher expectations;

- experience of bullying within school;

- the degree of participation in extra-curricular activities within the school.

The variables derived from the survey of schools are discussed in greater detail in Chapters 4 to 7.

2.3 ABILITY TESTING

A version of the Differential Aptitudes Test (DATS Tests in Verbal Reasoning and Numerical Ability) was administered by Department of Education psychologists to Junior Cert pupils in our sample. These two tests of verbal reasoning (VR) and numerical ability (NA) are drawn from a battery of six tests of cognitive skills for 15 year old pupils developed in the United States and adapted for Irish standards by the Educational Research Centre.

The tests were administered approximately three months before pupils sat their Junior Cert exam. Due to the initial over-sampling of community/comprehensive schools, ability testing was not carried out in nine schools in this sector. In addition, one school refused to co-operate with the testing. Within the schools tested, there was some shortfall in the numbers due to absentee-ism on the day of testing. These tests yielded complete informa-tion on 4,696 Junior Cert pupils, 79 per cent of the total sample or 93 per cent of sampled pupils within the schools involved in the testing. Test results were matched to the data from the pupil questionnaires using Department of Education pupil numbers.

Ability test scores were used as a proxy for the differences be-tween schools in the ability mix of their pupil intake. It would have been preferable to have information on pupils' abilities prior to their entry to second-level schooling since "effective" schools may enhance the test scores of their pupils. However, this was not feasible within the constraints of the *Coeducation and Gender Equality* study. In situations where national or local educational systems routinely conduct ability tests on second-level entrants, analyses have been conducted on the "value added" by the school to pupil performance, that is, the difference which attending a particular school or school type makes over and above the initial ability level of the pupil (see Gray, 1995; Hill, 1994). Other studies have used information on pupils' social background to assess the impact of schools on pupil performance without including controls for initial ability (see, for example, Croxford and Cowie, 1996). However, the latter approach may produce slightly different results than one using more complete information on pupil intake (Thomas and Mortimore, 1996). The issue of information requirements for analysing school effectiveness will be discussed in greater detail in Chapter 12.

This study will assess the influence of schooling processes, controlling for differences in family background among the pupil intake. The use of third year ability scores allows for a more detailed account to be taken of differences in pupil intake. Previ-ous analyses, using data from twenty-one schools for which first year ability scores were available, have indicated that third year scores represent a reliable proxy for first year scores (see Hannan, Smyth *et al.*, 1996).

2.4 EXAMINATION RECORDS

Examination results for Junior Cert and Leaving Cert pupils within the sampled schools were subsequently obtained from the Department of Education in September/October 1994. These results were matched to the pupil file using the Departmental pupil numbers. For the purposes of this study, we use the grade point average achieved for all pupils taking five or more subjects in the examination, with scores assigned using an adapted version of the Central Applications Office (CAO/CAS) marking scheme (see Hannan, Smyth *et al.*, 1996; Breen, 1986). In order to assess the degree of stability of school effects over time, 1996 examination data were subsequently collected for Junior and Leaving Certificate pupils in the sampled schools.

2.5 MEASURES OF SCHOOL EFFECTIVENESS

In general, studies of school effectiveness has focused on the impact of schooling processes on pupil performance measured using grades in national examinations, in the English and Scottish cases, or standardised ability test scores, in the American case (for exceptions, see Mortimore *et al.*, 1988; Bryk, Lee and Holland, 1993). In contrast, this study reflects the complex set of goals and tasks facing second-level schools by adopting a multi-dimensional approach to school effectiveness. A number of measures of pupil outcomes are used:

- Educational performance at Junior and Leaving Certificate levels, measured using the average grade received per examination subject;

- Pupil absenteeism, measured using teachers' reports of attendance records among Junior Certificate pupils; unfortunately no comparable information is available on Leaving Certificate pupils;

- Potential drop-out among Junior Certificate pupils, measured using pupils' reports of their intentions after the Junior Cert exam; this information was supplemented by school records on rates of pupil drop-out over the junior and senior cycles;

- Current stress levels among Junior and Leaving Cert pupils, measured using an adapted form of the conventionally used

General Health Questionnaire scale (see Hannan, Ó Riain, 1993);

- Academic self-image among Junior and Leaving Cert pupils, a measure of how pupils evaluate their own academic abilities;

- Locus of control among Junior and Leaving Cert pupils, a measure of the extent to which pupils believe they are in control of events;

- Body image among Junior and Leaving Cert pupils, that is, pupils' evaluations of the attractiveness of their own bodies and self-presentation to others.

This study assesses the impact of key features of school organisation and process on the above pupil outcomes. The focus on the multidimensional nature of school effectiveness allows us to examine whether schools are effective across a range of aspects, promoting educational attainment but also enhancing social development among pupils, for instance; or whether some schools optimise exam performance but at the expense of higher drop-out rates among low ability pupils or high stress levels among pupils.

2.6 MULTI-LEVEL MODELLING TECHNIQUES

Social systems frequently have a hierarchical organisation; for example, people (level 1) live within households (level 2) within local authority areas (level 3), and pupils (level 1) learn within schools (level 2). The existence of hierarchically organised data means that we need to take this hierarchy into account when analysing data (Goldstein, 1995). Traditional regression techniques have involved the assumption that there is no autocorrelation within the data; that is, that pupils represent independent observations, rather than being clustered within schools. This approach can be represented graphically in Figure 2.1.

Figure 2.1 represents the relationship between prior ability and exam performance among pupils in a sample of second-level schools.[1] Higher ability pupils do better in their exams than lower

---

[1] These data are illustrative only; findings from the survey of second-level schools in Ireland will be presented in Chapters 3 to 10.

FIGURE 2.1: REGRESSION MODEL

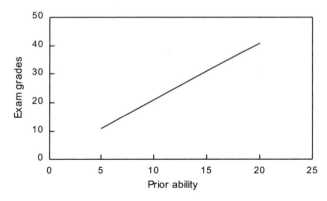

ability pupils and it is assumed that this relationship is universal, that is, that there are no "school effects". However, it cannot be assumed that pupils in the same school are completely "independent" of each other in this way. Groups rarely form at random and, once formed, the members of a group interact with each other to create even greater homogeneity (Jones, 1992). Treating pupils within a school as independent observations results in mis-estimated precision, incorrect standard errors, confidence limits and tests (Jones, 1991). Consequently, using regression techniques for research on schools increases the risks of finding differences and relationships where none exist[2] (Goldstein, 1995; Kreft and de Leeuw, 1998).

In contrast to regression procedures, *multi-level modelling* techniques take the clustering of individuals within groups into account. Figure 2.2 illustrates what is termed a "random intercepts" model. It indicates (as in Figure 2.1) that higher ability pupils do better in exams than lower ability pupils. However, it is also clear that schools differ from each other in the performance of their pupils; in this example, pupils in School 1 do consistently better than pupils in School 3 at each ability level.

---

[2] For example, using multi-level techniques, Aitkin and Longford (1986) found no significant differences in test scores due to teaching style whereas an earlier study using regression techniques had identified significant differences.

FIGURE 2.2: RANDOM INTERCEPTS MODEL

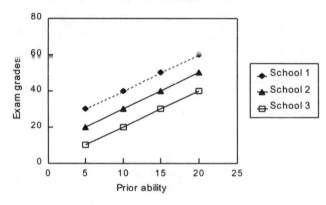

This approach can be developed further to allow the relationship between ability and performance to vary across schools; this is termed a "fully random" model. Figure 2.3 indicates that there is a much larger difference between the exam grades of lower and ability pupils in School 1 than in School 3. In addition, it is evident that schools make more of a difference for higher ability pupils. Later analyses will test whether the pattern in second-level schools in Ireland resembles that depicted in Figure 2.2 or Figure 2.3.

FIGURE 2.3: FULLY RANDOM MODEL

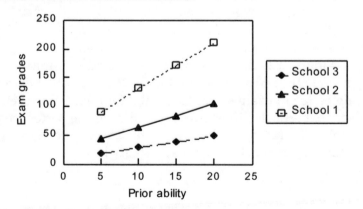

Analyses presented in this report were carried out using the MLn computer package developed in the Institute of Education, University of London (see Rasbash and Woodhouse, 1995; Woodhouse, 1995). Output from this package provides estimates of both fixed and random parameters and thus helps us to assess school effects in the following ways. First, we can assess the impact of pupil-level variables, such as gender, ability etc., on pupil performance.[3] Second, we can estimate the influence of school-level variables[4] (such as type of class allocation) on pupil performance, controlling for differences in pupil composition. MLn provides more precise estimates of the effects of school-level variables than traditional regression (see Appendix 2.1) and allows us to disentangle the influence of school organisation and policy from the effect of pupil composition. In terms of random parameters, MLn provides estimates of both school-level and pupil-level variance controlling for the specified fixed effects. The school-level variance term allows for the calculation of a residual for each school, which assesses the extent to which the school differs from the average, once differences in pupil intake are taken into account. This measure allows us to estimate the extent of variation between schools in pupil outcomes (see Chapters 4 to 7).

Multi-level modelling techniques have been found to yield significant technical and substantive benefits in conducting educational research (Goldstein and Spiegelhalter, 1996; Goldstein, 1997). The use of multi-level modelling techniques has recently become well established as a means of assessing the "value added" by schools to pupil performance, that is, the overall contribution the school makes to the development of each of its pupils (Hill, 1994).

2.7 SCHOOLS OR CLASSES?

There has been much discussion in the school effectiveness literature as to whether the focus for analysis should be the school, class or individual teacher (Creemers and Reezigt, 1996). Rowe and Hill (1994), for example, argue that between-classroom variation in achievement is more important than variation between schools. However, it should be noted that their research refers to primary schools where children had the same teacher for all subjects.

---

[3] The resulting estimates can be interpreted in the same way as conventional regression coefficients.

[4] School-level variables may be global (e.g. type of class allocation; type of curricular provision) or composite (that is, based on aggregate responses from pupils, such as average rating of the school as strict).

The approach used in this study is based on two levels: pupils (level 1) grouped within schools (level 2). While a three-level approach (pupils within classes within schools) would be illuminating, it is not feasible for the present study. First, many pupils in second-level schools have no "class" in any real sense. At Junior Cert level, 9 per cent of the sampled schools have only one "class" and, in one-third of the remainder, "classmates" are together for only three (or fewer) subjects. At Leaving Cert level, 23 per cent of the sampled schools have only one "class" and, in 88 per cent of the remaining schools, "classmates" are together for two (or fewer) subjects. Thus, a considerable proportion of pupils in the sampled schools, especially at Leaving Cert level, are with different groups of pupils for different subjects, especially where subjects are set or optional. To accurately capture these "class" effects would require the use of a very complex cross-classified model (see Rasbash and Woodhouse, 1995; Goldstein, 1997) where each pupil is simultaneously regarded as the member of up to nine class groupings and detailed information is available on each of these class groups.

Secondly, schools effects research is by its nature retrospective; pupils have been in the school for five to six years before we have information on their Leaving Cert results, for example, and their performance will reflect the conditions prevailing and their class membership over the whole of this period. They will have had many different teachers over their schooling career and the classes they have been part of will have been influenced by school-level decisions on subject availability and choice, class allocation and teacher allocation to classes and levels. Finally, in policy terms a focus on the whole school would appear to be more appropriate than a focus on individual teachers or classes. For these reasons, the focus of the study is on school-level factors while it is recognised that many of these factors operate by influencing effective teaching at the classroom level.

2.8 CASE-STUDIES OF SCHOOLS

Phase two of the study involved detailed case-studies of six schools in order to identify the complex of school organisation and process factors characteristic of more and less effective schools. Statistical analyses carried out in phase one of the study were used to identify "outliers", that is, schools that were significantly different from the average in terms of the pupil outcomes considered. This process is described in greater detail in Chapter 10. While other pupil outcomes were taken into account, the primary focus was on selecting schools in terms of their academic effectiveness, that is, schools were selected in terms of their residuals on academic performance, absenteeism and drop-out.

Efforts were made to ensure consistency in school effects. First, school residuals for English and Maths were compared with those for aggregate exam performance in 1994 so that only schools that had fairly consistent results across subjects would be selected. Second, residuals for Junior and Leaving Cert performance in 1994 were compared to ensure consistency between junior and senior cycle effects. Third, aggregate performance in 1994 was compared with that in 1996 to ensure some stability over time in school effects. In addition, other factors, such as school type, size, pupil intake and urban/rural location, were taken into account in selecting schools. Two "academically more effective" and two "academically less effective" schools were selected along with two "average" schools in order to provide a baseline for the interpretation of school differences.

Fieldwork for phase two of the study was carried out from March to May 1997. Detailed interviews were carried out with principals and vice-principals in the six schools. These interviews covered aspects of school organisation and process at the time of the interview (1997) along with changes in the school since the previous survey in 1994. Teachers in the school were interviewed about their perceptions of the students, their workload, their experience of in-service training and attitudes to working in the school. In total, 190 teachers in the six schools were interviewed. An effort was made to interview as many teachers (including guidance counsellors, home-school liaison co-ordinators and postholders) as possible, with response rates varying from 60 per cent[5] to 100 per cent. In addition, representatives from parents' associations were interviewed about their involvement in the school.

Studies of school effectiveness have rarely combined quantitative information from national (or regional) surveys of schools with qualitative information derived from more detailed case-studies of individual schools (for notable exceptions, see Sammons *et al.*, 1997; Teddlie and Stringfield, 1993). The use of such an approach in this study enhances our understanding of school

---

[5] The lower response rate in this school was due to the large number of part-time teachers teaching non-second-level courses.

effectiveness in a number of ways. First, the statistical analysis means that we can locate the six case-study schools within the national picture, identifying their relative effects on pupil outcomes. Second, the quantitative aspect of the study identifies factors associated with positive outcomes across all second-level schools. However, this represents only an "average" effect. The case-studies allow us to explore whether certain facilitating conditions are necessary for the success of certain policies and to discern some of the reasons for the implementation of such policies. Third, the case-studies involve interviews with teachers, yielding an additional perspective on school climate and issues such as staff-management relations. In overall terms, these case-studies allow us to take account of the complex way in which pupil and school factors interact "on the ground" to bring about positive or negative outcomes and to elaborate the broader analyses from the total sample of schools. The purpose of this research is not to evaluate individual schools but rather to identify models of good practice in school organisation and process which can inform policy and practice across all second-level schools. Findings from these case-studies are presented in Chapter 11.

2.9 SUMMARY

This chapter has outlined the research methodology used in the study. A number of aspects of the research design enhance its value as a study of effectiveness among second-level schools in Ireland. First, the large sample size means that the results are generalisable to the population of second-level schools and pupils in Ireland, and provide an accurate picture of the differences between schools in key features of organisation and process. Second, very detailed information has been collected on individual pupils as well as on school organisation and process. This level of detail allows us to compare "like with like" and thus provide an accurate estimate of the effects of schools on pupils' educational performance, absenteeism, drop-out and personal/social development. Third, the combination of quantitative and qualitative information allows us to identify general trends across the second-level sector while providing detailed information on how schools operate "on the ground".

Appendix

MULTI-LEVEL MODELLING TECHNIQUES

Multi-level models fall into two broad categories: random intercepts models; and fully random models. The simplest form of the
two-level random intercepts model is:

$$y_{ij} = \beta_j + e_{ij}$$
$$= \beta_0 + u_j + e_{ij} \qquad (1)$$

Here, y_{ij} is the grade point average (GPAV) of pupil i in school j;
this can be broken down into a school component β_j and a deviation (e_{ij}) for each pupil from her/his school's average. The school
component can be further broken down into the overall mean
GPAV across all schools β_0 and the deviation of each school from
that overall mean u_j; the latter can also be referred to as the
school-level residual. The model in (1) is in the same form as a
simple analysis of variance, although the estimation procedure
differs (see below). The two random terms $(u_j$ and $e_{ij})$ can be sum-
marised by their variances, σ_e^2 and σ_{u0}^2. The proportion of variability at the school level, or "intra-school correlation", is defined
as:

$$\sigma_{uo}^2 / (\sigma_e^2 + \sigma_{u0}^2) \qquad (2)$$

The intra-school correlation can be taken as an indicator of the
extent to which variation in a particular outcome is attributable
to the school level. If the measure is very small, we can conclude
that schools have little impact on pupil grade point average.

Model (1) can be extended to incorporate the impact of pupil
ability (x_1) on grade point average:

$$y_{ij} = \beta_0 + \beta_1 x_{1ij} + u_j + e_{ij} \qquad (3)$$

Now the school-level residuals (u_j) refer to the variation of schools'
performance from the overall mean, controlling for the ability
level of pupils in that school. The presence of this school-level
"error" term distinguishes a multi-level model from a conventional
regression model. The school-level residual is commonly used as

ness (see Hill, 1994); schools with large positive residuals can be seen as "effective" while schools with large negative residuals are deemed "ineffective". The model specified in (3) can be extended to incorporate other pupil-level variables (such as gender, social class etc.) along with school-level variables (such as school size etc.). Similar models of pupil performance are presented in Chapters 4 and 5.

A further development is possible by allowing the relationship between prior ability and grade point average to vary across schools, that is, a fully random model:

$$y_{ij} = \beta_0 + \beta_{1j} x_{1ij} + u_j + e_{ij}$$
$$\beta_{1j} = \beta_1 + u_{1j} \qquad\qquad (4)$$

In (4), there is the average relationship between ability and grade point average across all schools (β_1) and the deviation (u_{1j}) of each school from this overall slope. Similar models of differential effectiveness are presented in Chapter 8.

Multi-level models are also possible where outcomes are discrete rather than continuous variables (Goldstein, 1995) (see Chapter 6). In addition, a number of outcomes can be modelled simultaneously (see Chapter 9).

Analyses were carried out using the MLn computer package developed by the Institute of Education, University of London (Multilevel Models Project, 1995). MLn implements an Iterative Generalised Least Squares procedure. Initial estimates of the fixed terms are derived by Ordinary Least Squares techniques ignoring the higher-level random terms. The squared residuals based on this initial fit are then regressed on a set of variables defining the structure of the random part to provide initial estimates of the variance/covariances. These estimates are then used in a generalised least squares analysis to provide revised estimates of the fixed part, which is in turn used to revise the estimates of the random part, and so on until convergence (Jones, 1991; Goldstein, 1995).

Multi-level modelling techniques are found to have a number of technical advantages in the estimation of school effects:

1.   The multi-level approach explicitly takes autocorrelation into account, resulting in improved estimates of school-level variables, and correct estimates of standard errors, thus al-

lowing for the construction of valid confidence limits and tests.

2.   It allows for the possibility of heterogeneity at both higher and lower levels.

3.   Multi-level estimates are precision-weighted to reflect the number of observations on which they are based. Estimates are multiplied by a shrinkage factor whereby the estimated school mean moves towards the overall mean if there are few students in that school (Goldstein, 1997).

Chapter 3

ASPECTS OF SCHOOL ORGANISATION AND PROCESS

This chapter describes key aspects of school organisation and process in the sampled second-level schools. Discussion is grouped around seven areas: (i) school staffing and management; (ii) school organisation and class allocation; (iii) curriculum and subject choice; (iv) pupil involvement in the school; (v) parental involvement in the school; (vi) disciplinary climate; (vii) school interaction; and (viii) academic climate. The extent to which these characteristics influence pupil academic and personal development will be assessed in the following chapters.

3.1 SCHOOL STAFFING AND MANAGEMENT

Figure 3.1 indicates the ratio of pupils to full-time teachers within the 116 sampled schools; the majority of schools have a ratio of 17-18 pupils per full-time teacher. The average across all schools is 18 which is equivalent to the national figure (see *Key Education Statistics, 1984/85-1994/95*). The ratio of pupils to part-time teachers ranges from 11 to 926, with a median of 101. The latter figure should be interpreted with caution as it conflates teachers with very different hourly inputs. The variation in both full-time and part-time ratios does, however, reflect the different staffing strategies adopted by second-level schools.

The majority (70 per cent) of schools surveyed had experienced an increase in staffing levels over the five years prior to the interview (i.e., 1989-1994); one-fifth had stable levels, with one-tenth of schools experiencing an overall decline in staff numbers.

Principals were questioned about the school's approach to staff involvement and the division of labour within the school. One-third of schools hold formal staff meetings on a frequent basis, that is, one or more per month; 44 per cent hold two or more staff meetings per term. The majority (75 per cent) of principals consider these meetings to be very important, with only two principals stating these meetings are not important. Interestingly, reported frequency and perceived importance of staff meetings on the part of principals are not significantly related.

FIGURE 3.1: FULL-TIME PUPIL-TEACHER RATIO

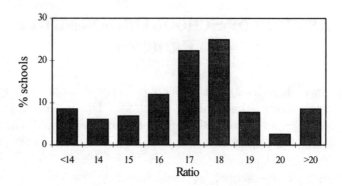

The number of senior management posts (Vice-Principal, A- and B-posts) ranges from one to thirty-two per school, with an average of 13.8 across schools. As expected, the number of management posts is related to the number of pupils within the school. Principals were asked about the type of tasks carried out by post-holders and these tasks were grouped into important management (e.g., head of team), significant authority (e.g., year head) and specific discrete (e.g., school equipment) functions. In over half (53 per cent) of schools, the Vice-Principal carries out important management functions; in two-thirds of schools s/he carries out significant authority functions while s/he carries out specific discrete functions in half of the schools surveyed. These categories are not mutually exclusive as a vice-principal may take responsibility for very diverse functions within the school. Involvement of A- and B-post holders in significant management functions is much less frequent, taking place in only 6 and 1 per cent of schools respectively. A-post holders have a high level of involvement in significant authority functions (78 per cent), while this is also the case for the majority of B-post holders (65 per cent). B-post holders are highly represented among specific discrete tasks; 86 per cent are involved in these tasks compared with 62 per cent of A-post holders. These measures were combined to give an overall measure of the division of labour in the school. Only a very small minority (6 per cent) of schools involved both A- and B-posts in the important management functions of the school. A more usual pattern was to confine important management functions to the Vice-Principal only or to involve all post-holders in significant authority functions within the school. Where A- and/or B-post holders are involved in management functions, formal staff meetings tend to be viewed as less important by the principal, most likely because other channels of communication exist between staff. In general, school principals tend to view the operation of A- and B-posts as "successful" or "very successful" with greater dissatisfaction expressed by those in secondary schools compared with other school types.

3.2 SCHOOL ORGANISATION AND CLASS ALLOCATION

Schools with more than one class per year group generally use one of three approaches in allocating pupils to classes. *Streaming* involves the grouping of pupils of similar levels of assessed academic ability into the same classes; these classes are ranked in terms of average pupil ability from "top" to "bottom" class. Some form of random allocation process (such as alphabetical listing) is usually used in the case of *mixed ability* allocation, although, in a few cases, schools specifically aim to produce a mix of ability by actively dispersing pupils of different levels of assessed ability between the various classes. *Banding* is practised in many larger schools. This entails dividing pupils into broad ability bands; each of these bands is then further subdivided into classes on the basis of mixed ability (usually involving some form of random allocation).

Figure 3.2 indicates the use of ability-based differentiation by year group and school sector. The use of banding/streaming is less prevalent in the entry year indicating that many schools tend to postpone decisions about pupil allocation until they have more complete information on pupils' academic performance. Ability-based differentiation is more commonly used in vocational and community/comprehensive schools than in secondary, particularly coed secondary, schools. Streaming/banding is less commonly used at Leaving Cert level, usually because there are fewer classes and pupils have a greater choice of subjects (see Hannan, Smyth *et al.*, 1996).

FIGURE 3.2: ABILITY-BASED DIFFERENTIATION BY SCHOOL ODOTOR

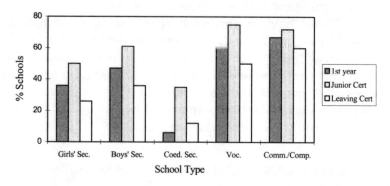

Note: Figure refers to schools with more than one base class.

The system of class allocation used has important implications for pupils' access to particular subjects and levels within subjects. Four systems for determining access to higher, ordinary or foundation levels are available to schools: (i) mixed ability/common level, where pupils taking different subject levels are taught within the same class; (ii) full setting, where pupils move to different classes depending on the level they are taking; (iii) restricted setting, where pupils from certain base classes only can move to higher or ordinary level classes;[1] and (iv) allocation, where the level at which a pupil takes a subject is determined by their base class.

Table 3.1 presents the systems used by schools for Irish, English and Maths at Junior Cert level. Over half of second-level schools use full setting for Irish, English and Maths at Junior Cert level; that is, pupils can move from one class to another depending on the level they are taking in a particular core subject.[2] Full setting in Irish, English and Maths is obviously more prevalent in schools with mixed ability base classes and therefore more common in coed and girls' secondary schools. Almost one-quarter of schools provide setting in at least one other subject, usually a language or science. Full mixed ability or com-

---

[1] The usual situation is that the top and middle classes can take honours or ordinary level, with the bottom/remedial classes allocated to ordinary or foundation level.

[2] Full setting refers to base classes only; schools can also impose criteria for access to higher level subjects for individual pupils on the basis of past performance (see Hannan, Smyth *et al.*, 1996).

mon level teaching is less common, taking place in about one-sixth of schools. Streamed/banded schools tend to use restricted setting or allocation, limiting access to higher level subjects to top and sometimes middle classes. Comparing systems across subjects, restricted setting is found to be more common in Maths than in the other subjects. Differences between schools in how subject levels are made available to pupils may have important implications for academic performance among pupils (see Chapter 4).

TABLE 3.1: ACCESS TO SUBJECT LEVELS FOR JUNIOR CERT IRISH, ENGLISH AND MATHS

System	Irish	English	Maths
	%	%	%
Mixed ability	15.5	16.4	12.1
Full setting	53.4	51.7	55.2
Restricted setting	14.7	13.8	17.2
Allocation	16.4	18.1	15.5
N	116	116	116

Full setting is much more prevalent at the Leaving Cert level, with over two-thirds of schools using such a system for the "core" subjects (Irish, English and Maths) (see Table 3.2). Full setting is more prevalent in coed and girls' secondary schools than in other school types. Just under half (45 per cent) of second-level schools provide setting in at least one other exam subject, with the total number of subjects set ranging from none (11 per cent of schools) to fifteen. Allocation is much more rarely used than at Junior Cert level; where schools have streamed/banded classes, they tend to use restricted setting systems.

TABLE 3.2: ACCESS TO SUBJECT LEVELS FOR LEAVING CERT IRISH, ENGLISH AND MATHS

System	Irish	English	Maths
	%	%	%
Mixed ability	13.4	12.5	12.5
Full setting	68.8	67.9	68.8
Restricted setting	14.3	16.1	17.0
Allocation	3.6	3.6	1.8
N	112	112	112

3.3 CURRICULUM AND SUBJECT CHOICE

Table 3.3 indicates that there is a substantial degree of variation between schools in the way subjects are made available to pupils. A small proportion (4 per cent) of schools provide no choice of subjects for the Junior Certificate. The number of exam subjects taken and the relative proportion of core and optional subjects differ from school to school.[3] The number of optional subjects is strongly related to school size, with larger schools providing fewer core and more optional subjects. Within schools, mixed ability and top classes tend to take more exam subjects at Junior Cert level than middle or bottom/remedial classes (Table 3.3). Thus, the class allocation system influences not only the level at which subjects are taken but also the number of subjects taken.

TABLE 3.3: NUMBER OF EXAM SUBJECTS BY TYPE OF CLASS

	Junior Cert		Leaving Cert	
	Mean	Range	Mean	Range
Mixed ability class:				
Core	6.5	4-9	3.2	3-8
Options	2.7	0-5	3.9	0-5
Total	9.2	6-11	7.2	7-9
Top class:				
Core	6.8	4-11	3.1	2-5
Options	2.3	0-5	4.0	2-5
Total	9.1	8-11	7.1	7-8
Middle class:				
Core	6.2	5-10	3.1	3-4
Options	2.3	0-4	3.9	3-4
Total	8.5	7-10	7.0	7
Bottom / remedial class:				
Core	6.3	3-9	3.2	2-5
Options	2.4	0-5	3.8	1-5
Total	8.7	6-10	7.0	6-8

---

[3] "Core" subjects refer to the subjects which are obligatory for particular base classes within a particular school.

Schools vary in the timing of Junior Cert subject choice; a small minority of schools require pupils to choose subjects before entry, almost half allow for subject choice over the entry year, while 43 per cent postpone choice until entry to second year. Later subject choice is more prevalent in single-sex secondary schools than in the other school sectors. The packaging of options changes regularly in almost half of the sampled schools while over one-third of schools provide no choice or have not changed the options for more than five years. These measures are related, that is, schools tend to be (in)flexible in relation to both the timing and the variation in subject choice.

There is very little evidence of curricular specialisation at Junior Certificate level. Some differences between schools are evident in relation to the provision of technical subjects, languages (excluding French) and traditionally "female" subjects (such as Home Economics); there are also a small number of schools which do not provide the mainstream "academic" subjects (History, Geography, French) (see Hannan, Smyth *et al.*, 1996 for further details).

There is less variation between schools in the number of Leaving Cert exam subjects taken with the vast majority of pupils taking seven exam subjects. Only one school in the sample provides no choice of subjects for Leaving Cert. Over one-quarter of schools require pupils to choose subjects before Easter of Junior Cert year, while one-fifth of schools postpone subject choice until after pupils receive their Junior Cert results. Subject choice tends to occur somewhat earlier in community/comprehensive schools than in other school types, perhaps because of the logistical problems associated with greater average school size. Optional packages change regularly in three-quarters of schools although one-tenth have not changed their subject packages for more than five years.

In terms of curricular provision, the vast majority of schools provide at least one science (including higher level Maths), commerce, modern languages, arts, or history/geography subject. In contrast, a sizeable minority of schools do not provide technical subjects or home economics (see Hannan, Smyth *et al.*, 1996). Schools vary in the size of their curriculum (excluding Irish, English and Ordinary Maths), with thirteen subjects representing the most frequent pattern. An index of subject specialisation, a measure of the extent to which curricular provision could be seen as general or specialised, was derived (see Hannan, Breen *et al.*,

1983). Schools differ in the extent of subject specialisation, with larger schools and/or those providing a larger number of subjects giving more scope for subject specialisation. Boys' secondary schools tend to have the highest level of specialisation with coed secondary and vocational schools providing the most general curricular mix.

3.4 PUPIL INVOLVEMENT IN THE SCHOOL

The measure of formal pupil involvement reflects the existence of student councils or prefect systems within the school. Pupil involvement was found to be relatively high in one-quarter of schools, with no formal involvement in one-third of schools. A lack of formal involvement is more common in vocational schools than in other school types while girls' secondary schools have the highest level of such involvement. Pupil involvement also tends to be higher in larger schools and is positively related to the frequency of staff meetings within the school, both factors which would tend to indicate a more participative school climate.

Informal involvement among pupils in their school tends to be low. Over half of Junior Cert pupils and 60 per cent of Leaving Cert pupils had no involvement in school-based sports, societies, debates or plays in the two weeks prior to the interview. Average participation in such extra-curricular activities varies significantly between schools, however, with the highest level of involvement found in secondary, particularly coed secondary, schools.

3.5 PARENTAL INVOLVEMENT IN THE SCHOOL

A number of different aspects of parental involvement were assessed: parental involvement in subject choice; participation in parent-teacher meetings; and the existence of a parents' association. All of this information is based on principals' reports. More detailed information from the perspective of school management, teachers and parents' association representatives in the six case-study schools is presented in Chapter 11. At junior cycle, parents have little or no involvement in subject choice in almost one-quarter of schools, with high involvement (with information sent from the school to parents and formal meetings regarding subject choice) in under one-third of schools. A high level of involvement is more apparent at Leaving Cert level where just under half of the schools involve parents in subject choice through meetings. At both junior and senior cycle levels, vocational schools are least likely, and girls' schools most likely, to involve parents in subject choice. As might be expected, parental involvement is more common where subject decisions are taken later and where pupils have a greater number of optional subjects.

All of the sampled schools report periodic parent-teacher meetings, although the majority of schools hold such meetings only once a year for each year group. Schools vary in the proportion of parents who would normally attend, with an average reported attendance of 75 per cent. Combining frequency and attendance levels gives a measure of parental involvement in parent-teacher meetings; involvement is found to be higher[4] in secondary schools than in vocational and community /comprehensive schools.

The vast majority (83 per cent) of schools have a parents' association or council; boys' secondary and vocational schools are somewhat less likely than other school types to have such a body. These associations may vary in the role they play within the school (see Chapter 11).

3.6 DISCIPLINARY CLIMATE

School principals were asked to assess the frequency of pupil misbehaviour within their school (see Table 3.4). In general, reports of serious misbehaviour are rare. Principals in boys' secondary and vocational schools tend to report somewhat higher levels of pupil misbehaviour than those in other school types.[5]

Pupils were asked to rate their school along the dimension "strict"–"easy going". Around half of the schools were rated as being "in-between" in terms of strictness with one-quarter described as strict; Junior Cert pupils were more likely to consider their school easy-going than their Leaving Cert counterparts. Girls' schools were most likely to be described as strict by their pupils while pupils in boys' and vocational schools were more likely to describe their school as easy-going.

---

[4] In other words, parent-teacher meetings are held more frequently and are attended by a greater proportion of parents.

[5] However, principals of girls' schools report a higher incidence of bullying and truancy than those in other school types, an interesting pattern given the lower incidence of bullying reported by female pupils in the sample.

TABLE 3.4: PUPIL MISBEHAVIOUR BY SCHOOL SECTOR (PRINCIPAL'S REPORT)

	Boys' Secondary	*Girls' Secondary*	*Coed Secondary*	*Vocational*	*Community/ Comprehensive*
Classroom misbehaviour[1]	38.9	15.4	15.0	38.2	16.7
Persistent misbehaviour[2]	71.8	42.3	50.0	55.8	55.6
Serious misbehaviour[2]	16.7	7.7	5.0	17.6	5.6
Bullying[2]	33.3	76.9	55.0	51.5	61.1
Truancy[2]	44.5	67.2	40.0	58.8	61.2
N	18	26	20	34	18

Notes: [1] Per cent reporting frequent; [2] Per cent reporting frequent/occasional.

Principals were asked about homework policy in the school; the majority reported clear rules regarding the setting, doing and checking of homework. In addition, pupils were questioned about their usual experience of homework procedures. The most frequent pattern involves pupils checking their homework in discussion with the teachers, although this pattern is somewhat less prevalent at Leaving Cert level. Around one-tenth of pupils report that their homework is not usually checked. The type of approach used varies across school types, with girls' secondary schools more likely to allow pupils to check their own homework in consultation with teachers. Those in bottom/remedial classes are more likely than those in other classes not to have their homework checked.

3.7 TEACHER-PUPIL INTERACTION

There tends to be a relatively high level of satisfaction with school among pupils; around three-quarters of Junior and Leaving Cert pupils agree or strongly agree with the statement that "for the most part, school life is a happy one for me". At the pupil level, girls, middle-class pupils and higher ability pupils tend to be more satisfied with school. Schools vary in the overall satisfaction levels of their pupils; ratings range from 38 to 100 per cent satisfied at Junior Cert level and 40 to 92 per cent at Leaving Cert level. Average pupil satisfaction is higher in schools that are seen as organised and/or friendly schools by their pupils. It is positively related to a high level of positive interaction, and a low level of negative interaction, with teachers. Satisfaction ratings are highest in girls' secondary schools and lowest in vocational schools.

Pupils were questioned about the extent of positive and negative interaction with teachers within the school. Girls and boys report equal levels of positive interaction[6] but girls report less negative interaction with teachers and bullying by other pupils than boys. Individual schools vary significantly in the overall level of positive interaction, negative interaction and bullying by other students.

3.8 ACADEMIC CLIMATE

Schools may vary in their emphasis on, and support for, academic achievement among teachers and pupils. The academic climate of the school can be assessed by examining pupil orientations towards study and teacher expectations (as reported by pupils). At Junior Cert level, pupils spend an average of 3.5 hours per night on homework/study. Schools vary from each other in terms of the average time spent by pupils on study, with school-level averages ranging from 2 to 4.5 hours. Variation at the class level is somewhat greater than at the school level, perhaps reflecting class streaming/banding practices. Study hours are associated with the formalisation of homework rules at the school level, that is, pupils tend to spend more time on homework/study where a school has clear rules about the setting and checking of homework.

Much of the school effectiveness literature has focused on the role of teacher expectations in shaping pupil outcomes (see Chapter 1). However, different aspects of academic emphasis by teachers should be distinguished: teachers' expectations in relation to exam performance, as perceived by pupils; the highest educational level expected by teachers; and (at Junior Cert level)

---

[6] This pattern should be interpreted with some caution. Classroom observation studies indicate that teachers spend more time giving positive feedback to boys (see, for example, Drudy and Ní Chatháin, 1996). Girls' reports in our study may reflect lower expectations in relation to teacher interaction.

whether teachers expect pupils to leave school after the Junior Cert.[7]

TABLE 3.5: TEACHER EXPECTATIONS OF PUPIL PERFORMANCE

| | Junior Cert | | Leaving Cert | |
	Girls	Boys	Girls	Boys
Very well	33.9	25.4	22.4	18.7
Well	60.1	63.3	67.8	64.1
Just below average	5.5	9.0	8.0	13.2
Well below average	0.6	2.3	1.8	4.0
N	2,980	2,905	2,490	2,266

The majority of pupils at both Junior and Leaving Cert levels report that their teachers expect them to do "well" in the forthcoming exam (Table 3.5). Girls report significantly higher teacher expectations than boys. Pupils who report higher teacher expectations also tend to report more positive interaction with teachers. The average level of teacher expectations differs significantly between schools.

TABLE 3.6: TEACHER EXPECTATIONS OF EDUCATIONAL LEVEL AND DROP-OUT

| | Junior Cert | | Leaving Cert | |
	Girls	Boys	Girls	Boys
Level:				
Junior Cert	8.0	11.1	1.1	1.7
Leaving Cert	36.9	44.0	20.7	28.7
Diploma	32.9	27.3	35.7	32.4
Degree	22.2	17.6	42.5	37.2
Drop-out (%)	1.5	4.8	-	-
N	2,980	2,905	2,490	2,266

The vast majority of Junior Cert pupils report that their teachers expect them to obtain a Leaving Cert or higher with one-fifth reporting degree-level expectations (Table 3.6). At Leaving Cert level, the majority of pupils report that their teachers expect them

---

[7] These measures are based on pupil reports aggregated to the school level. It would have been preferable to obtain information directly from teachers on their expectations for pupils. This issue will be explored in the case-studies of schools (see Chapter 11).

to go on to further education, including 40 per cent who are expected to get a degree. Only a very small number of pupils report that their teachers expect them to drop out of school. Girls report higher teacher expectations of third-level participation and lower expectations of drop-out than boys. Although the proportion is low at the pupil level, the school-level aggregate measure of expected drop-out varies from 0 to 50 per cent. The pattern relating to third-level expectations also varies between schools.

At the aggregate level, schools characterised by low teacher expectations in relation to exam performance have higher expected drop-out rates. However, there is no relationship with the average educational level expected by teachers. This may mean that "high" expectations are relative (in the view of pupils and/or teachers); teachers in some schools may expect their pupils to do "well, considering".

3.9 CONCLUSIONS

Compared to other systems, the Irish educational system is highly standardised in terms of curriculum and examinations (Hannan, Raffe, Smyth, 1996). However, it appears that there is substantial discretion at the individual school level regarding key aspects of school organisation and process. This chapter has indicated that schools vary significantly in their systems of class allocation, degree of subject choice, level of pupil and parental involvement, disciplinary climate, nature of interaction, and academic climate. The extent to which these aspects of school policy and ethos influence academic and personal development among pupils will be examined in Chapters 4 to 7.

Chapter 4

JUNIOR CERTIFICATE EXAM PERFORMANCE

This chapter examines the effects of school organisation and process on pupil performance in the Junior Certificate examination. Given the existence of nationally standardised examinations in the Irish context, exam results serve as an important indicator of educational "output". Formal exam results are frequently used by employers in recruitment decisions (Breen, Hannan and O'Leary, 1995). Although fewer young people now leave school directly after the Junior Certificate (McCoy, Whelan, 1996), Junior Cert exam results also play an important role in access to particular subjects and subject levels in the senior cycle (Hannan, Smyth *et al.*, 1996).

4.1 JUNIOR CERTIFICATE GRADE POINT AVERAGE

Junior Certificate performance is measured in terms of grade point average (GPAV), that is, pupils are assigned a score for each grade they achieve in their exam and the scores are averaged across all exam subjects taken. The scoring system used is presented in Table A4.1 and the following analyses relate to pupil performance in 1994. There has been much discussion in the school effectiveness literature about whether the focus should be on aggregate exam performance or on performance in individual subjects (see, for example, Sammons *et al.*, 1997). The following analyses focus on aggregate performance for a number of reasons. First, overall exam performance plays an important role in securing access to paid employment and to further education. Second, such an approach allows us to focus on the whole school as an organisation rather than on particular subject departments or teachers. Third, aggregate exam performance is likely to be more stable over time than exam results in individual subject areas (see Sammons *et al.*, 1997). It is, however, recognised that school effects may vary across different subjects, although such an investigation lies outside the parameters of the current study.

TABLE 4.1: JUNIOR CERT GRADE POINT AVERAGE (GPAV) BY
SCHOOL SECTOR AND GENDER

	Single-sex Secondary		Coed Secondary		Vocational		Community/ Comprehensive	
	Boys	Girls	Boys	Girls	Boys	Girls	Boys	Girls
GPAV	6.7	7.1	6.5	7.0	5.4	5.8	5.7	6.4
Average VRNA	52.7	48.0	50.4	47.5	37.4	38.0	41.4	41.8
Average social class	2.7	3.0	2.8	2.8	3.5	3.7	3.3	3.2

Note: Weighted by gender and ability mix within the school.

Table 4.1 indicates Junior Cert results by school sector and
gender; these are "raw" results, that is, exam scores have not been
adjusted to take account of any background or ability differences
between pupils in the various school types. Girls are found to outperform boys at Junior Certificate level within each of the school
types. Exam performance varies by school sector with lower
performance among pupils in vocational schools and higher performance among those in secondary schools. However, school
sectors also differ in terms of pupil composition; working-class and
lower ability pupils are disproportionately concentrated in the vocational sector. The extent to which school type differences reflect
differences in pupil composition will be explored later in the chapter.

The remainder of this chapter presents a series of multi-level
models analysing the impact of pupil and school characteristics on
pupil performance, as measured by Junior Cert grade point average. The explanatory variables used in these models are
described in Table A4.2. The following analyses are unweighted;
additional analyses weighting data to allow for the differential
sampling of schools and pupils do not differ substantially from
estimates based on unweighted data.

TABLE 4.2: MULTI-LEVEL MODELS OF JUNIOR CERT GRADE POINT AVERAGE (N=5,191)

Fixed effects	Model 1	2	3	4	5
Intercept	6.443	6.708	6.550	6.556	6.385
Pupil background:					
Gender (female)		.488*	.585*	.592*	.820*
Social class		-.260*	-.115*	-.107*	-.106*
Social class unknown		-1.688*	-.770*	-.747*	-.747*
Mother's education		.175*	.054*	.049*	.048*
Parental education unknown		-.912*	-.341*	-.340*	-.350*
Aged 16 and over		-1.153*	-.472*	-.464*	-.468*
Ability:					
VRNA score			.135*	.134*	.134*
VRNA squared			-.001*	-.001*	-.001*
Missing for ability test			-.718*	-.719*	-.719*
School context:					
Average social class				-.284*	-.343*
School type:					
Coed Secondary					.069
Coed Secondary* Girls					-.143
Vocational					.304*
Vocational* Girls					-.334*
Comm./Comp.					.224
Comm./Comp. *Girls					-.268
Random effects:					
School-level variance	0.892*	0.423*	0.161*	0.130*	0.122*
Pupil-level variance	3.110*	2.642*	1.284*	1.283*	1.282*
Deviance[1]	20902.1	19999.5	16229.9	16209.2	16200.2
Degrees of freedom	-	6	9	10	16
Improvement in deviance	-	<.001	<.001	<.001	n.s.

Note: * denotes significance at the <.05 level;
[1] The deviance statistic is equal to -2 (log-likelihood); a reduction in the deviance statistic indicates an improvement in the fit of the model.

The average grade per subject for Junior Cert pupils is 6.4, the equivalent to just over a B grade on an ordinary level paper

(Model 1, Table 4.2). The variance terms indicate the extent to which individual schools and pupils within these schools vary around this average. It is found that the "intra-school correlation" is 0.223, that is, 22 per cent of the total variance in exam performance is attributable to the school level (Table 4.3). The school-level variance term is significant, indicating that schools differ significantly from each other in their "raw" Junior Cert exam performance. The variance term can be used to calculate a residual for each school, that is, a measure of the extent to which exam performance in a given school differs from the overall average. The extent of this difference is presented graphically in Figure 4.1 for the 106 schools included in the Junior Cert analyses.[1] It is clear that there are substantial differences between schools; the highest-performing school outperforms the lowest-performing school by 4.5 grades per subject, averaging a higher level C grade per subject compared to an ordinary level D grade per subject for the lowest-performing school.

FIGURE 4.1: "RAW" SCHOOL DIFFERENCES IN JUNIOR CERT GPAV

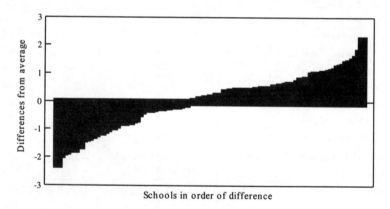

Schools in order of difference

4.2 PUPIL BACKGROUND FACTORS

Junior Certificate performance is strongly influenced by the background characteristics of pupils. Girls outperform boys by almost half a grade, even controlling for social background and age (see Model 2, Table 4.2). Social class has a significant influence on

---

[1] The following analyses exclude the ten schools for which ability test scores were not available.

grade point average; pupils from a higher professional background score 1.3 grades per subject higher than those from an unskilled manual background.[2] The "social class unknown" term is significant, with these pupils achieving over 1.6 grades per subject less than those from the higher professional class; this could reflect greater disadvantage among this group (such as under-reporting of parental occupation where parents are long-term unemployed) or alternatively may reflect incomplete answers to the questionnaire on the part of lower ability pupils. Mother's education[3] also has a significant effect on pupil performance; pupils with mothers who attended university score 0.7 grades per subject higher than those whose mothers only had a primary education. The "parental education unknown" term shows a similar negative effect to "social class unknown", indicating lower performance among pupils who fail to report parental education. Those who are older than average (16 years of age or older) do significantly worse in the Junior Cert than their younger counterparts. This group is likely to contain a disproportionate number of pupils who were "kept back" a year or more over their time in primary or second-level school and thus the pattern is likely to reflect a longer-term process of educational under-achievement. Pupil background, gender and age account for over half of the difference between schools in average performance (see Table 4.3).

Pupils sat verbal reasoning and numerical ability (VRNA) tests approximately three months before their Junior Cert exams. It would have been preferable to have had intake measures of pupil ability in order to fully assess the impact of school characteristics on subsequent performance. However, previous analyses

---

[2] Here social class is treated as a continuous variable (see also Hannan, Smyth *et al.*, 1996). Alternative analyses representing class as a series of dummy variables yield very similar estimates of inter-class performance differences.

[3] Mother's education is used in preference to father's as it is more highly correlated with pupil performance.

TABLE 4.3: VARIANCE EXPLAINED BY DIFFERENT MODELS OF
JUNIOR CERT PERFORMANCE

Model	School-level variance explained	Pupil-level variance explained	Intra-school correlation
	%	%	
Null model	-	-	0.223
Pupil background[1]	52.6	15.0	0.138
Background + ability	81.9	58.7	0.111
Background, ability + social context	85.4	58.7	0.092
Background, ability, context + school type	86.3	58.8	0.087
Background, ability + school organisation/ process	90.4	67.1	0.078

Note: [1] This includes gender and age.

(see Hannan, Smyth *et al.*, 1996) indicated that these test scores
could be taken as a broadly reliable proxy of differences in ability
on intake.[4] It should be noted that using third-year ability scores
will tend to result in an under-estimate of school effects on pupil
outcomes. Therefore, significant effects identified are likely to be
even stronger if intake measures were used.

FIGURE 4.2: PRIOR ABILITY AND JUNIOR CERT PERFORMANCE

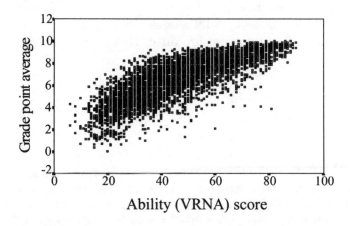

Ability (VRNA) score

---

[4] This conclusion was based on analyses of the twenty-one schools in the
sample for which intake measures were available.

Pupils who had higher scores on the ability tests tend to do better in the Junior Certificate exams (Model 3, Table 4.2). The VRNA squared term indicates that the relationship between prior ability and performance is somewhat flatter at the higher ability levels, showing a ceiling effect for the returns to prior ability[5] (see Figure 4.2). Those pupils who were missing from school on the day of the ability test have significantly lower than average exam scores. This is likely to reflect a lower average ability level among absentees and possibly the direct effect of absenteeism on exam performance, an issue which will be explored in subsequent chapters. Pupil background and prior ability account for over half (58 per cent) of the difference between pupils in Junior Cert exam performance. They also account for most (82 per cent) of the variation between schools in average performance (Table 4.3). However, significant differences remain between schools even when differences in pupil intake are taken into account.

4.3 SCHOOL SOCIAL CONTEXT

The social class mix (average social class) within a school has a significant impact on pupil performance (Model 4, Table 4.2). Pupils in predominantly middle-class schools tend to have higher exam scores than those in predominantly working-class schools, even when their own social background is taken into account. School social context explains an additional 3.5 per cent of the variation in average performance between schools (Table 4.3). Figure 4.3 indicates the difference in exam performance between schools when we control for pupil background, prior ability and social context. The extent of school differences is markedly reduced compared to that in "raw" school results (see Figure 4.1). In addition, the ranking of individual schools in terms of their average performance changes when pupil composition is taken into account. Thus, some schools boost the performance of even low ability pupils while others do relatively badly given their high ability intake; this issue will be explored further in Chapter 10. The disparity between raw and adjusted exam scores indicates the problems with relying on a crude "league table" approach in analysing school differences since knowing a school's raw score tells

---

[5] There is a maximum (an A grade at higher level) to the grades a pupil can achieve; in addition, it may be more difficult for a pupil to increase performance from a B to an A grade than from a D to a C grade.

us little about the amount of progress pupils in a given school make relative to their initial ability level (see Goldstein and Spiegelhalter, 1996). Significant differences between schools in adjusted exam results are apparent and there is a difference of 1.4 grades per subject between the highest and lowest-performing schools (Figure 4.3). While significantly less than the raw differences, these differences between schools are likely to have substantive effects on pupils' subsequent educational and occupational chances.

FIGURE 4.3: ADJUSTED SCHOOL DIFFERENCES IN JUNIOR CERT GPAV

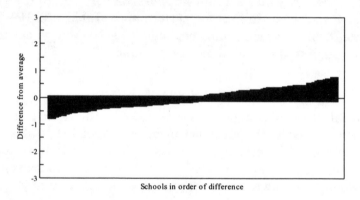

Schools in order of difference

4.4 SCHOOL TYPE

Table 4.1 indicated the difference between school sectors in Junior Cert exam performance. When pupil background, prior ability and social context are taken into account, there are no significant performance differences between coed secondary, single-sex secondary and community/comprehensive schools. However, controlling for social context, vocational schools appear to boost performance for boys but not for girls. This boost for boys in vocational schools is only apparent when social mix of the school is taken into account, that is, boys in vocational schools do better than would be expected given the high concentration of working-class pupils in these schools. However, there are no significant differences between the vocational sector and other school types when only individual pupil background and prior ability are taken into account. School type, therefore, tells us little about differences between schools in average exam results. It is necessary to turn to aspects of school organisation and process in order to explore the reasons for these differences.

TABLE 4.4: SCHOOL FACTORS AND JUNIOR CERT PERFORMANCE

	Model					
Fixed effects	*1*	*2*	*3*	*4*	*5*	*6*
School organisation:						
Streaming	-.153*	-.109	-.078	-.064	-.042	-.036
Class allocation:						
Top class	.586*	.549*	.516*	.511*	.522*	.451*
Middle class	-.108	-.150	-.178	-.173	-.174	-.161
Bottom/remedial class	-.539*	-.580*	-.611*	-.614*	-.613*	-.535*
Involvement:						
Pupils-formal		.146*	.078	.048	-.021	-.022
Subject choice flexible		.158*	.177*	.174*	.078	.093
Disciplinary climate:						
Strict school			.193*	.172*	.056	.051
Pupil behaviour			.408*	.409*	.238*	.266*
School Interaction:						
Average positive interaction				.442	.055	.024
Average negative interaction				-.880*	-.848*	-1.033*
Academic climate:						
Average teachers' expectations					.776*	.489*
Teacher expectations						.182*
Pupil aspirations						.360*
Random effects:						
School-level variance	0.210*	0.185*	0.156*	0.135*	0.091*	0.086*
Pupil-level variance	1.170*	1.170*	1.170*	1.170*	1.170*	1.022*

Note: * p<.05.

All models are controlled for pupil background and ability. The coefficients for pupil background and ability factors are reported in Table A4.3.

4.5 SCHOOL ORGANISATION

Table 4.4 presents a series of multi-level models analysing the effects of school organisation and process on Junior Cert exam performance. Because social class context is highly correlated with a number of school characteristics, it is not included in these models. This approach allows us to explore the aspects of school process which potentially mediate the social class context of the school.

Streaming is found to have a significant negative impact on average pupil performance (see Table 4.4, Model 1). Pupils in highly streamed schools score over 0.6 grades per subject lower than those in schools with mixed ability base classes. Class allocation within streamed/banded schools has an additional impact. Pupils in top classes score over half a grade higher, and those in bottom classes half a grade lower, than those in mixed ability classes, all else being equal. Being in a middle class has a slight negative but statistically insignificant effect. Figure 4.4 shows the difference in average performance between the different class types. It is evident that, for pupils in highly streamed schools, even those in the top class have no advantage over those in mixed ability schools[6] while those allocated to the bottom class underperform significantly relative to their initial ability.

FIGURE 4.4: JUNIOR CERT GPAV BY CLASS TYPE

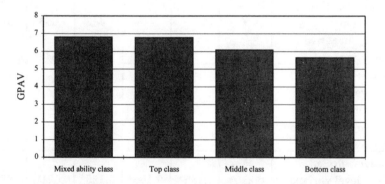

Further analyses were carried out to assess whether these differences are due to the type of class grouping system employed (see Chapter 3). The boost for the top class is apparent whether schools allocate subject levels to classes, or use restricted or full setting; however, the effect is slightly stronger where allocation and restricted setting are used. The negative effect of being in a bottom/remedial class is apparent for all system types, although

---

[6] This occurs because the effect of being in a highly streamed school (4 x -0.153) cancels out the boost from being in the top class (+0.586).

the negative effect is particularly strong where subject levels are allocated. In other words, pupils in bottom classes do worse in the Junior Cert in part because they have little or no access to higher level courses. Other factors, such as poorer perceptions of their own ability and lower teacher expectations, may also play a part. Where base classes are mixed ability, the use of setting has a somewhat positive but statistically insignificant effect. This effect should be interpreted with some caution since very few schools use "pure" mixed ability teaching across all subjects.

Other aspects of school organisation, such as school size and pupil-teacher ratio, were found to have no significant impact on pupil performance. The lack of effect of pupil-teacher ratio does not imply that class size has no substantive impact on educational outcomes but is likely to reflect the small degree of variation in pupil-teacher ratios across the second-level sector in Ireland (see Chapter 3). The crucial factor is likely to be the way in which particular schools use their teaching resources rather than the pupil-teacher ratio *per se*.

4.6 INVOLVEMENT IN THE SCHOOL

The extent of formal involvement of pupils in the school has a significant positive effect on pupil performance (Model 2, Table 4.4). Thus, pupils do better academically in schools where they are given positions of responsibility within the school structure. In contrast, informal pupil involvement (the extent of participation in extracurricular activities) has no significant effect on performance at Junior Cert level.

Parental involvement in subject choice is positively associated with performance but is not included in the model due to its high correlation with a number of the other variables. Similarly, high involvement in parent-teacher meetings has a slightly positive effect on Junior Cert results.

A more flexible approach to subject choice has a positive effect on exam performance; pupils tend to do better in schools where subject choice is delayed, perhaps until entry to second year. In overall terms, pupils tend to do better academically in schools where they (and their parents) experience some sense of ownership and control over school life.

4.7 DISCIPLINARY CLIMATE

Pupils tend to obtain higher exam grades in schools which are characterised as strict by the pupils. A similar effect is apparent for pupils' perceptions of how organised the school is, but this factor is not included in the final models due to intercorrelation with other factors. The effect of formal pupil involvement is no longer significant when strictness and pupil behaviour are entered (Model 3, Table 4.4). This means that pupils' formal involvement is greater in strict schools and that its effect on their exam results is being mediated by disciplinary climate. Exam results are better where incidences of pupil misbehaviour are rare, as reported by the school principal. In addition, pupils tend to do slightly worse in exams when their homework is not regularly checked. In summary, pupils tend to do better academically where there is a stronger disciplinary climate in the school, where they experience fewer disruptions to their learning time through pupil misbehaviour, and where they undergo regular monitoring of their school work.

4.8 TEACHER-PUPIL INTERACTION

The nature of relationships between teachers and pupils in a school has a significant effect on pupil performance. Average positive interaction (as reported by pupils) is positively associated with exam results, although the effect is just below statistical significance. In contrast, the level of negative interaction between teachers and pupils is strongly associated with lower levels of exam performance (Model 4, Table 4.4). Pupils in schools with higher levels of negative interaction obtain lower exam grades, even when their personal experience of negative interaction is taken into account. In addition, the average level of satisfaction with school life was analysed; this is positively associated with performance, but not included in the final model due to high correlations with other variables. Taken together with the findings on disciplinary climate, it would appear that a "strict but fair" school climate is optimal for pupil performance. Pupils tend to do better where they view the school as strict but an overly or unfairly strict school (where a high proportion of pupils feel they are regularly "given out to" by teachers) has negative effects on achievement.

4.9 ACADEMIC CLIMATE

The level of teacher expectations within a school (as perceived by pupils) has a positive and significant impact on pupil performance. In other words, pupils tend to do better in exams when teachers in the school expect most pupils to go on to the Leaving Certificate and/or higher education (see Model 5, Table 4.4). The effects of average positive interaction and strictness are reduced in effect, indicating that the nature of pupil-teacher relations and the disciplinary climate contribute to the creation of a high expectational climate within the school. It could be argued, however, that this finding merely reflects the fact that pupils who themselves intend to remain in education report that their teachers intend them to stay on. This was assessed in Model 6 (Table 4.4) which controls for pupils' own level of educational aspirations and their individual reports of their teachers' expectations. Pupils who expect to stay on in full-time education tend to do better than those with lower aspirations. This pattern is likely to reflect two inter-linked processes. First, pupils who do not intend to stay on in full-time education have fewer incentives to study to achieve higher grades. Second, lower educational aspirations on the part of some pupils are likely to reflect previous experiences of educational failure or underperformance. Pupils do better in their exams where their teachers expect them to stay on in education, even controlling for pupils' own expectations. However, the school-level average of teacher expectations still has a positive and significant effect; that is, pupils tend to do better in schools which are characterised by a pervasive climate of high expectations.

Figure 4.5 represents the relationships among the factors included in the model. It is not intended to represent a causal model as in many cases the causal processes in operation are likely to be more complex. Pupil background has a direct effect on exam performance, but the effect is partially mediated by prior ability and pupil aspirations. Girls, middle-class pupils and those of average age do better in the Junior Cert in part because they are more likely to intend to go on to higher education. Academic climate mediates the effect of a number of other dimensions of school organisation and process. In other words, schools with a positive expectational climate also tend to be characterised by a more flexible approach to subject choice, a stricter disciplinary code and

FIGURE 4.5: RELATIONSHIPS AMONG PUPIL BACKGROUND, SCHOOL PROCESS AND EXAM PERFORMANCE

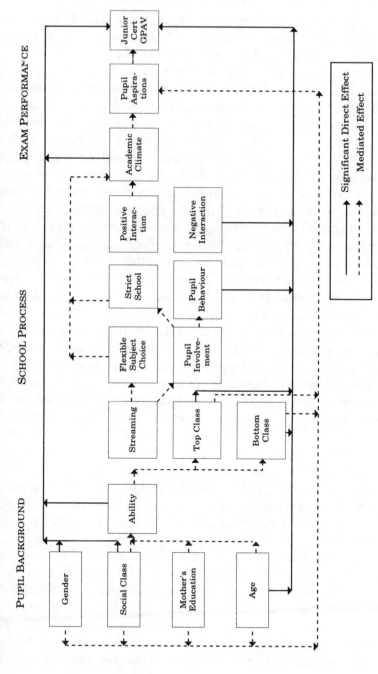

more positive interaction between teachers and pupils. In turn, academic climate has a direct positive effect on pupil performance but also has an indirect effect by promoting higher aspirations among pupils.

Taking account of the specified features of school organisation and process significantly reduces the predicted differences between schools in average Junior Certificate performance. The vast majority (90 per cent) of performance differences between schools are accounted for by pupil background, prior ability and school organisation/process. These factors also explain a good deal (67 per cent) of the variation between pupils in exam results (Table 4.3).

The analyses reported in this chapter and represented in Figure 4.5 focus on the impact of school characteristics on the "average" pupil. Therefore, it is assumed that the key features of school organisation identified in this study have similar effects on girls and boys, pupils from different social class backgrounds, and those of different ability levels. The extent to which this is a valid assumption will be discussed in Chapter 8.

4.10 STABILITY IN SCHOOL EFFECTS

It has been argued that the performance of schools is likely to vary significantly from year to year, thus making estimates of school effects unreliable (see Chapter 1). Ideally, the stability of school effects would be tested by conducting separate multi-level analyses using detailed pupil- and school-level information for a range of years and pupil outcomes (see, for example, Sammons *et al.*, 1997). Unfortunately, this is not possible within the constraints of the current study. However, it is possible to examine the relationship between schools' academic performance in two different years, and to take account of pupil composition (albeit in an earlier year) in assessing the impact of schools on Junior Certificate performance.

Examination data for 1996 were compared to data for the sample year, 1994; due to closures and amalgamations, data could only be collected for 111 schools. There is a very high correlation (r = 0.91) between overall ("raw") grade point average in 1994 and 1996, that is, schools that had higher average performance in 1994 tend to have higher performance in 1996. When separate subjects are considered, the correlation between the two years is 0.87 for English and 0.90 for Maths, a pattern which is consistent with British findings that overall performance is more stable over time than performance in individual subjects (Sammons *et al.*, 1997).

When schools are ranked in terms of their performance in 1994, 7 out of the "top 10" schools in 1994 are still ranked in the top 10 in 1996. Similarly, of the bottom 10 schools in 1994, 8 are still in the bottom group in 1996. However, a crude "league table" approach tells us nothing about the effects of schools over and above the impact of pupil composition.

Because of the absence of pupil-level data for 1996, a full multi-level analysis of school effects on pupil performance cannot be conducted. However, a school-level regression using composite pupil variables from 1994 can be carried out; such an analysis must be interpreted with some caution due to the difficulties of working at the aggregate level only (see Goldstein, 1995). For comparative purposes, these analyses were carried out for both 1994 and 1996.

TABLE 4.5: REGRESSION OF 1994 AND 1996 JUNIOR CERT PERFORMANCE ON PUPIL COMPOSITION

Explanatory variables	1994	1996
Intercept	4.901	5.281
School type:		
Boys' school	-.393**	-.448**
Girls' school	.436***	.528***
Pupil composition:		
Average social class	-.371***	-.389**
Average VRNA score	.063***	.056***
Average unemployment	-.016**	-.017**
R^2	0.817	0.734

Note: *** $p<.001$; ** $p<.01$

For 1994, average pupil performance at the school level was regressed on aggregate pupil composition and school type. Girls' schools had significantly higher, and boys' schools considerably lower, average grades than coed schools. The results for boys' schools should be interpreted with caution. Since girls outperform boys at Junior Cert level (see Table 4.2 above), the presence of girls in coed schools will boost the aggregate grade point average compared to that in boys' schools. Performance is influenced by pupil composition: average social class, average ability and average proportion of pupils with unemployed parents. These compositional factors account for 82 per cent of the variance in Junior Cert performance across schools. Thus, the aggregate analyses for the 1994 Junior Cert results reflect similar processes to, but without the complexity of, the multi-level models described earlier in the chapter.

Exam data for 1996 were regressed on pupil composition factors drawn from the 1994 survey. The assumption is that the mix of pupils (in terms of social composition and ability) is unlikely to change significantly from year to year; this assumption will be tested below by comparing Junior and Leaving Cert survey data. Pupil composition (social class, parental unemployment, gender) in 1994 explains a high proportion (67.1 per cent) of the variance in Junior Cert performance in 1996. When average ability (of the 1994 cohort) is included, 73.4 per cent of the variance is explained by pupil composition. Thus, pupil composition (in 1994) remains highly predictive of exam results two years later.

In terms of stability, pupil exam performance (in raw terms) is highly correlated across years. There seems to be some movement in the placement of individual outlier schools[7] when pupil composition is taken into account but there is a relatively high correlation ($r = 0.6$-0.7) between school-level residuals for 1994 and 1996. There is a relative lack of specificity about what constitutes "stability" in school effects but these correlations are somewhat below those found in a sample of schools in inner city London (Sammons *et al.*, 1997). Systematic data on pupils and schools over time would be needed in order to reach more definitive conclusions about the stability of school effects (see Gray *et al.*, 1995).

4.11 CONCLUSIONS

A large proportion of the difference in average Junior Certificate performance between schools is due to differences in the background characteristics of pupils within the school. Girls, middle-class pupils and those with highly educated parents tend to do better in the Junior Certificate exam. As in other studies (e.g. Croxford and Cowie, 1996; Paterson, 1991), an additional contextual effect is found; that is, pupils in predominantly middle-class

---

[7] Outlier schools are those with exam performance significantly above or below the average.

schools tend to do better in the Junior Cert than those in predominantly working-class schools, even taking their own social
background and ability into account. While taking account of
differences in pupil intake reduces the amount of variation
between schools, substantive differences in average exam
performance are still evident among second-level schools.

A number of aspects of school organisation and process are
found to have significant effects on pupil outcomes. Streaming has
significant negative consequences on average but underperformance is particularly evident among those allocated to bottom
classes within the school. This pattern is partly related to these
pupils' lack of access to higher level courses but may also relate to
lower expectations on the part of pupils and/or teachers. Second,
pupils tend to do better in the Junior Certificate where they experience some sense of control over their school life either through
formal involvement in the school or through more flexible choices
in relation to subject take-up. Third, a "strict but fair" school
climate appears to be optimal for pupil performance; pupils tend
to do worse where their school is too "easy-going", where pupil
misbehaviour disrupts their learning time, or where they feel
teachers are not interested in them or are constantly "giving out"
to them. Fourth, the academic climate of the school plays an
important role in enhancing academic progress; pupils tend to do
better in exams where their teachers expect them to stay on in
full-time education. These key features of schooling, in conjunction with pupil background and ability factors, explain almost all
of the difference between schools in average Junior Certificate
performance. The extent to which these factors continue to influence academic progress over the senior cycle will be assessed in
the next chapter.

Appendix

TABLE A4.1: ALLOCATION OF POINTS TO JUNIOR CERTIFICATE GRADES

Grade	Higher level	Ordinary level	Foundation level
A	10	7	4
B	9	6	3
C	8	5	2
D	7	4	1
Other	0	0	0

TABLE A4.2: EXPLANATORY VARIABLES FOR JUNIOR CERTIFICATE GRADE POINT AVERAGE

Variables	Description
Pupil Background	
Gender	Dummy variable where 1= Girl.
Social class	Census Social Class scale ranging from 0 (Higher Professional) to 5 (Unskilled manual worker) based on the occupational status of parents.
Social class unknown	Dummy variable where 1= Social class not reported.
Mother's education	Highest level of mother's education ranging from 0 (primary education) to 4 (university degree).
Parental education unknown	Dummy variable where 1= Mother's (or father's) education not reported.
Aged 16 and over	Dummy variable where 1= Aged 16 or more on 1st January 1994.
Ability / Performance	
Ability	VRNA, combined verbal reasoning and numerical ability scores; centred on its mean value.
Missing for ability test	Dummy variable where 1= Absent from school on day of VRNA test.

School social context	
Average social class	Average social class of pupils within the school; centred on its mean value.
School organisation	
Streaming	Extent of streaming and associated curricular differentiation in the school; Guttman scale ranging from 0 (mixed ability base classes) to 4 (highly streamed).
Top class Middle class Bottom class	Set of dummy variables where 1= in top, middle or bottom/remedial class respectively; contrasted with membership of mixed ability base class.
Involvement	
Formal pupil involvement	Level of formal involvement by pupils in the schools; ranges from 0 (low) to 2 (high).
Subject choice flexible	Timing of subject choice; ranges from 0 (no choice) to 3 (subject choice made on entry to second year).
Disciplinary climate	
Strict school	School-level average of pupil rating of school as "strict"-"easy-going"; centred on its mean value.
Pupil behaviour	Scale compiled from principal's report of frequency of discipline problems; centred on its mean value.
School Interaction	
Average positive interaction	School-level average of positive teacher-pupil interaction; centred on mean.
Average negative interaction	School-level average of negative teacher-pupil interaction; centred on mean.
Academic climate	
Average teacher expectations	School-level average of the highest qualification which teachers expect the pupil to get. Ranges from 1 (Junior Cert) to 4 (University Degree); centred on its mean value.
Teacher expectations (individual pupil report)	Highest qualifications which teacher(s) expect the pupil to get; ranges from 0 (Junior Cert) to 3 (university degree).
Educational aspirations	Highest qualifications which the pupil expects to get; ranges from 0 (Junior Cert) to 3 (university degree).

TABLE A4.3: MULTI-LEVEL MODELS OF JUNIOR CERT GPAV (SCHOOL PROCESS)

Explanatory Variables	Model					
	1	2	3	4	5	6
Intercept	6.806	6.247	6.239	6.253	6.510	5.681
Pupil background:						
Gender (female)	.480*	.466*	.457*	.440*	.446*	.264*
Social class	-.101*	-.101*	-.101*	-.102*	-.097*	-.067*
Social class unknown	-.670*	-.686*	-.684*	-.690*	-.681*	-.561*
Mother's education	.049*	.048*	.048*	.048*	.045*	.005
Parental education unknown	-.288*	-.292*	-.292*	-.288*	-.289*	-.268*
Aged 16 and over	-.427*	-.425*	-.423*	-.427*	-.423*	-.339*
Ability:						
VRNA score	.109*	.108*	.108*	.108*	.108*	.100*
VRNA squared	-.0004*	-.0004*	-.0004*	-.0004*	-.0004*	-.0005*
Missing for ability test	-.691*	-.692*	-.692*	-.692*	-.692*	-.596*
School organisation:						
Streaming	-.153*	-.109	-.078	-.064	-.042	-.036
Class allocation:						
Top class	.586*	.549*	.516*	.511*	.522*	.451*
Middle class	-.108	-.150	-.178	-.173	-.174	-.161
Bottom/remedial class	-.539*	-.580*	-.611*	-.614*	-.613*	-.535*
Involvement:						
Pupils- formal		.146*	.078	.048	-.021	-.022
Subject choice flexible		.158*	.177*	.174*	.078	.093
Disciplinary climate:						
Strict school			.193*	.172*	.056	.051
Pupil behaviour			.408*	.409*	.238*	.266*
School Interaction:						
Average positive interaction				.442	.055	.024
Average negative interaction				-.880*	-.848*	-1.033*
Academic climate:						
Average teachers' expectations					.776*	.489*
Teacher expectations[1]						.182*
Pupil aspirations[1]						.360*
Random effects:						
School-level variance	0.210*	0.185*	0.156*	0.135*	0.091*	0.086*
Pupil-level variance	1.170*	1.170*	1.170*	1.170*	1.170*	1.022*
Deviance	15782.5	15769.5	15753.5	15741.4	15706.4	15015.0
Degrees of freedom	13	15	17	19	20	24
Improvement in deviance[2]	<.001	<.01	<.001	<.01	<.001	<.001

Note: * $p < .05$;

[1] Dummy variables for missing information on these variables were included in the analysis but are not reported here.

[2] For model 1, this represents improvement over the null model (Model 1, Table 4.2). For the other models, the comparison is with the previous model.

Chapter 5

LEAVING CERTIFICATE EXAM PERFORMANCE

Chapter 4 examined the impact of a range of school organisation and process factors on pupil performance in the Junior Certificate examination. This chapter examines whether similar factors influence Leaving Certificate performance. In recent years, Leaving Cert exam results have assumed an increasingly crucial role in securing access to employment and further education. In this study, Leaving Cert performance is measured in terms of grade point average (GPAV), that is, "points" are assigned to exam grades and the scores averaged over all exam subjects. The scoring system used is described in Table A5.1. The following analyses relate to Leaving Cert exam performance in 1994.

5.1 LEAVING CERTIFICATE EXAM PERFORMANCE

Table 5.1 indicates that Leaving Certificate exam performance differs between school sectors. Girls are found to outperform boys at the Leaving Cert level, although the gap is smaller than at Junior Cert level. The pattern of variation by school sector is similar to that found at the Junior Cert, with pupils in secondary schools securing the highest grades and those in vocational schools the lowest grades. The following analyses will examine whether these sectoral differences hold when variation in pupil composition is taken into account.

The remainder of this chapter presents a series of multi-level models assessing the impact of pupil and school characteristics on exam performance; explanatory variables included in these models are described in Table A5.3. The estimates presented are based on unweighted data as weighted estimates do not differ substantially from those reported here.

TABLE 5.1: LEAVING CERT GRADE POINT AVERAGE BY SCHOOL TYPE AND GENDER

	Single Sex Secondary		*Coed Secondary*		*Vocational*		*Community/ Comprehensive*	
	Boys	*Girls*	*Boys*	*Girls*	*Boys*	*Girls*	*Boys*	*Girls*
GPAV	8.0	8.6	7.5	8.9	6.2	6.0	7.2	7.6
Prior JC performance[1]	6.8	7.0	6.4	7.0	6.0	5.9	6.6	6.9
Average social class	2.7	2.9	2.7	2.9	3.3	3.5	3.0	3.2

Note: [1] The scoring system for junior cycle performance is presented in Table A5.2.

The average grade per subject for all Leaving Certificate pupils is 7.8, that is, between a B3 and a B2 grade on an ordinary-level paper (Model 1, Table 5.2). The variance terms indicate that pupils differ significantly from each other in terms of their performance and that schools vary significantly in the average performance of their pupils. One-fifth of the total variance in pupil performance can be attributed to schools, slightly less than is the case for Junior Cert performance (Table 5.3). The difference between the 111 schools included in the analysis is presented graphically in Figure 5.1. The highest-performing school in the sample differs from the lowest-performing school by over 8 grade points per subject, the difference between a C3 on a higher level paper and a C3 grade on an ordinary level paper.

FIGURE 5.1: "RAW" SCHOOL DIFFERENCES IN LEAVING CERT GPAV

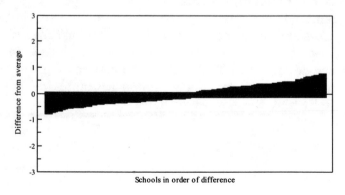

TABLE 5.2: MULTI-LEVEL MODELS OF LEAVING CERT GRADE POINT
AVERAGE (N=4,716)

	Model				
Fixed effects	*1*	*2*	*3*	*4*	*5*
Intercept	7.800	7.987	7.821	7.862	7.776
Pupil background:					
Gender (female)		.905*	.225*	.215*	.363
Social class		-.519*	-.119*	-.103*	-.102*
Social class unknown		-2.840*	-.326	-.280	-.268
Mother's education		.436*	.157*	.144*	.142*
Parental education unknown		-1.474*	-1.093*	-1.110*	-1.114*
Aged 18 and over		-.681*	.163	.164	.162
Prior Performance:					
Junior Certificate GPAV			2.056*	2.047*	2.046*
Junior Cert GPAV unknown			-2.259*	-2.254*	-2.264*
Intermediate Certificate			1.700*	1.594*	1.589*
Repeating Leaving Certificate			1.596*	1.647*	1.640*
School context:					
Average social class				-.655*	-.609*
School type:					
Coed Secondary					.148
Coed Secondary* Girls					.095
Vocational					.032
Vocational* Girls					-.165
Comm./Comp.					.101
Comm./Comp.* Girls					-.441
Random effects:					
School-level variance	3.737*	2.184*	0.716*	0.579*	0.576*
Pupil-level variance	15.120*	14.130*	5.443*	5.441*	5.433*
Deviance	26454.5	26088.5	21576.2	21555.3	21548.0
Degrees of freedom	-	6	10	11	17
Improvement in deviance	-	<.001	<.001	<.001	n.s.

Note: * p<.05.

5.2 PUPIL BACKGROUND

Girls outperform boys by almost a grade per subject at the Leaving Certificate level, even controlling for their age and family background (Model 2, Table 5.2). As at the Junior Cert, social class has a significant effect on pupil performance; there is a difference of over 2.5 grades per subject between pupils from a higher professional background and those from an unskilled manual background. The "social class unknown" group scores slightly lower grades than those from an unskilled manual background. Mother's education has an additional positive effect on exam grades; pupils whose mothers had a university education score 1.7 grades per subject more than the children of mothers with a primary education. Those who do not report their parents' education have significantly poorer exam results than others; this may reflect the under-reporting of low levels of parental education and/or a failure among lower ability pupils to adequately understand and respond to the questionnaire. Pupils who are older than average (aged 18 or over) tend to do worse in the Leaving Cert than their younger counterparts. Taking account of pupil composition (gender, social background and age) tends to reduce the extent of school-level variation; that is, over 40 per cent of the difference in average performance between schools is related to the gender, age and family background of their pupils (Table 5.3).

Performance in the Junior and Leaving Certificates are very closely related (r = 0.8) since they tend to reflect the same sorts of abilities and the same underlying processes. Model 3 (Table 5.2) enters prior performance in the Junior Cert into the model explaining Leaving Cert. This does not imply that Junior Cert performance directly affects Leaving Cert performance[1] but this approach allows us to assess the extent of pupils' academic progress over the senior cycle. Once Junior Cert performance is entered into the model, the other coefficients reflect the impact of particular factors on pupil progress between the Junior and Leaving Certificate. The relationship between performance and progress is complex. A pupil may have relatively low Junior Cert grades but may make good progress over the senior cycle, given her/his prior performance. However, s/he will not necessarily

---

[1] Junior Cert performance, however, may have an indirect influence on Leaving Cert performance by affecting the subjects and levels to which pupils have access at senior cycle (see Hannan, Smyth *et al.*, 1996).

secure higher Leaving Cert grades than their fellow pupil who had higher Junior Cert grades and made only average progress over the senior cycle, given their initial performance. This pattern may hold at the school level also; an individual school may boost the progress of pupils over the senior cycle, but only given relatively low grades at Junior Cert. The relationship between Junior and Leaving Cert performance and progress in individual schools will be explored in greater detail in Chapter 10.

Junior Cert GPAV is found to be highly predictive of performance at Leaving Cert level (Model 3, Table 5.2). For every grade achieved in the Junior Cert, a pupil could be expected to score two grade points in the Leaving Cert; the large value of the coefficient reflects the greater differentiation of grades ("A1", "A2" etc. as opposed to "A", "B" etc.) at Leaving Cert level. Those who do not report their Junior Cert results tend to do somewhat worse in their Leaving Cert than those with average Junior Cert grades; this may reflect a slight tendency among these respondents to under-report low grades. Around one-tenth of the sample had taken the Intermediate rather than the Junior Certificate examination and hence junior cycle exam scores differ for this group (see Table A5.2). The Inter Cert term corrects for differences in scoring between the Junior and Inter Cert exams, but does not have substantive significance. Those who are repeating the Leaving Cert make more progress (by 1.6 grades per subject) over the senior cycle than those sitting the exam for the first time, controlling for age.

The interpretation of the background effects changes once junior cycle performance is taken into account. Girls significantly outperform boys, controlling for their Junior Cert performance; that is, girls make more progress over the senior cycle relative to their initial ability than boys (Model 3, Table 5.2) as well as having higher overall grades in absolute terms (Model 2). Pupils from a middle-class background and those whose mothers have higher levels of education make more progress over the senior cycle, as well as securing higher grades overall. Age of pupil is no longer significant when prior performance is controlled for; that is, older pupils tend to do worse in their Leaving Cert but are not significantly different from other pupils in the amount of progress they make over the senior cycle. This pattern is evident only among those taking the Leaving Cert for the first time since those repeating the exam tend to do somewhat better than average. Pupil background and prior performance explain a very high proportion (81 per cent) of the difference between schools in average Leaving Cert performance (Table 5.3).

TABLE 5.3: VARIANCE EXPLAINED BY DIFFERENT MODELS OF LEAVING CERT PERFORMANCE

Model	School-level variance explained	Pupil-level variance explained	Intra-school correlation
	%	%	
Null model	-	-	0.198
Pupil background	41.6	6.5	0.134
Background + prior performance	80.8	64.0	0.116
Background, performance + social context	84.5	64.0	0.096
Background, performance, context + school type	84.6	64.1	0.096
Background, performance + school organisation/process	89.7	68.4	0.074

5.3 SCHOOL SOCIAL CONTEXT

The social class mix of a school has a significant impact on Leaving Cert grades. Those in predominantly working-class schools tend to make less progress over the senior cycle, relative to their performance at the Junior Cert level (Model 4, Table 5.2). Pupil background, prior performance and social context explain a very high proportion (84 per cent) of the difference between schools in average Leaving Cert performance. Significant differences remain between schools, however, with the highest progressing school differing from the lowest progressing school by almost four grade points per subject, the difference between averaging a higher level D2 and a lower level C1 grade (see Figure 5.2). This may represent a substantive difference for pupils, for example, in access to higher education and/or employment.

FIGURE 5.2: ADJUSTED SCHOOL DIFFERENCES IN
LEAVING CERT GPAV

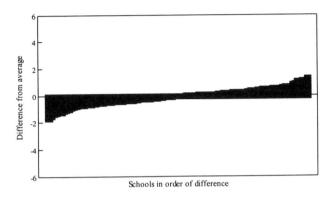

5.4 SCHOOL TYPE

The differences between school sectors apparent from Table 5.1
are no longer significant when account is taken of gender, family
background and prior performance (see also Breen, 1986). There is
some variation in exam scores between school sectors but none of
the differences are statistically significant (Model 5, Table 5.2).
Therefore, the raw grade differences reported between pupils in
the different school types (see Table 5.1) reflect differences in the
gender, social class and ability mix of the pupil intake rather than
a sectoral effect *per se*.

5.5 SCHOOL ORGANISATION

Streaming is less prevalent among Leaving Certificate classes
than among junior cycle classes (see Chapter 3). Contrary to the
Junior Cert pattern, streaming is found to have no significant
impact on the progress pupils make over the senior cycle (Model 1,
Table 5.4). In addition, the boost to performance found among
Junior Cert pupils in top classes is no longer apparent at the
Leaving Cert level; the coefficient is negative but these pupils do
not differ significantly from those in mixed ability base classes.
Being in a middle class has a negative effect on pupil perform-
ance, although the effect is just below statistical significance.

TABLE 5.4: SCHOOL FACTORS AND LEAVING CERTIFICATE GPAV

	Model					
Fixed effects	1	2	3	4	5	6
School organisation:						
Streaming	.032	.019	.023	.023	.053	.003
Top class	-.164	-.166	-.147	-.084	-.009	.089
Middle class	-.621	-.624	-.601	-.544	-.515	-.394
Bottom/remedial class	-.891*	-.898*	-.876*	-.814*	-.775*	-.401
Involvement:						
Pupils- formal		.257	.296	.278	.089	.064
Pupils- informal		.612*	.640*	.650*	.486*	.448*
Curriculum:						
Flexible subject choice			.238*	.261*	.210*	.151
Subject specialis-ation			.142*	.132*	.128*	.100*
School Interaction:						
Average negative interaction				-1.082	-.644	-.678
Academic climate:						
Average teachers' expectations					1.020*	.526*
Teacher expect-ations						.817*
Pupil aspirations						.711*
Random effects:						
School-level variance	0.686*	0.630*	0.580*	0.556*	0.475*	0.383*
Pupil-level variance	5.405*	5.404*	5.403*	5.404*	5.405*	4.771*

Note: * $p < .05$.

All models are controlled for pupil background and ability. The coefficients for pupil background and prior performance factors are reported in Table A5.4.

Being in a bottom class, however, has a significant negative effect on pupil progress over the senior cycle; pupils in bottom/remedial classes score almost one grade point per subject lower than those in mixed ability base classes, relative to their prior performance. This is of particular concern given the pattern found among Junior Cert pupils. Little is known in the Irish context about the extent to which pupils allocated to bottom classes for the junior cycle remain in these classes over their second-level career. However, if pupils remain in a bottom class over the whole of their second-level education, this is likely to result in a pattern of cumulative underperformance, relative to their ability levels.

5.6 INVOLVEMENT IN THE SCHOOL

There is a positive relationship between pupils' formal involvement in the school and their senior cycle progress, although the effect is slightly below statistical significance (Model 2, Table 5.4). The level of informal involvement among pupils is significantly related to Leaving Cert performance and progress. Thus, pupils tend to do better in schools where they are integrated into the formal and informal structures of the school. There is some tendency for enhanced progress to be associated with parental involvement in subject choice, although the effect is not statistically significant.

5.7 DISCIPLINARY CLIMATE

Junior Cert performance is found to be positively related to the disciplinary climate of the school (see Chapter 4). At Leaving Cert level, pupils' perceptions of the school's strictness is positively related to exam *performance* but not to senior cycle *progress*. A similar pattern is found in relation to the principal's perception of pupil (mis)behaviour, with a positive influence on performance but no significant impact on progress over the senior cycle.

5.8 CURRICULUM

As at Junior Cert level, pupils tend to make more academic progress in schools where there is a more flexible approach to subject choice, that is, where choices are made later rather than earlier (Model 3, Table 5.4). In addition, the degree of subject specialisation in a school is associated with enhanced pupil progress. This may arise because of some synergy between certain subject groupings. Thus, learning may be maximised where pupils are taking a number of science subjects, for example; alternatively, school specialisation may allow for the fostering of greater expertise in particular subject areas among the teaching staff. However, this grade advantage must be balanced against the consequences for subsequent educational participation and career choice of over-specialisation in subject take-up at second-level.

5.9 PUPIL-TEACHER INTERACTION

The average level of positive interaction between teachers and pupils in a school is not included in the model as it has no discernible impact on academic progress at senior cycle. However, individual experiences of positive interaction with teachers do help to explain differences among pupils within schools rather than differences between schools. In contrast, the extent to which relationships between teachers and pupils in a school are poor on average is significantly associated with pupil progress;[2] pupils make less progress in schools where there is a high degree of negative interaction with teachers (Model 4, Table 5.4).

5.10 ACADEMIC CLIMATE

As at Junior Cert level, the academic climate within a school has a significant impact on pupil progress. Pupils tend to do better in schools where most pupils are expected to go on to further education (Table 5.4, Model 5). As expected, pupils do better where they themselves expect to go on to further education, and where their teacher(s) expect them to do so (Model 6, Table 5.4). However, the aggregate effect of high teacher expectations persists when these pupil-level variables are taken into account; that is, high overall expectations among staff in a school help to boost pupil progress, even controlling for pupils' own educational aspirations.

Additional analyses were carried out to test whether variations in school effects reflect external factors, such as take-up of grinds on the part of pupils. Among the sample of Leaving Cert pupils, almost one-third had taken grinds or private tuition in the three months prior to the survey. Take-up of grinds is found to have a positive association with Leaving Cert performance but this effect disappears when educational aspirations on the part of pupils are taken into account. In other words, pupils who take grinds do better academically because they are more likely to intend to go on to higher education rather than because of the grinds *per se*. Allowing for grind take-up does not affect the amount of variation between schools or the ranking of schools in terms of average performance indicated in Figure 5.2 above.

Figure 5.3 represents the relationships among different aspects of school organisation and process. While social class and mother's

---

[2] This relationship is significant at the p<.10 level.

education have direct effects on exam performance, much of the effect of pupil characteristics is mediated through pupil aspirations. In other words, girls and middle-class pupils tend to do better because they are more likely to intend to go on to higher education. Pupil aspirations also mediate the effect of being in a bottom class and of pupil involvement, that is, those allocated to a bottom class tend to have lower aspirations while those who are actively involved in the school (through extra-curricular activities) tend to have higher aspirations. Pupil aspirations also partially mediate the effect of academic climate; pupils tend to develop higher educational aspirations in schools where there is a positive expectational climate and consequently they tend to do better academically. Academic climate mediates the effect of negative pupil-teacher interaction on pupil performance, that is, pupils in schools where teachers regularly "give out" to them tend to see teachers as having lower expectations for them which in turn reduces the amount of academic progress they make over the senior cycle.

Taking account of these key features of school organisation/process, in conjunction with pupil background and prior performance, explains most (90 per cent) of the variance between schools in average Leaving Certificate performance. In addition, over two-thirds (68 per cent) of the variance between pupils in exam performance is explained by this combination of factors. The models presented in this chapter focus on the impact of school characteristics on the "average" pupil; analyses presented in Chapter 10 will assess the extent to which school effects may differ for boys and girls, pupils from different social classes and of different ability levels.

FIGURE 5.3: RELATIONSHIPS AMONG PUPIL BACKGROUND, SCHOOL PROCESS AND
EXAM PERFORMANCE AT LEAVING CERT

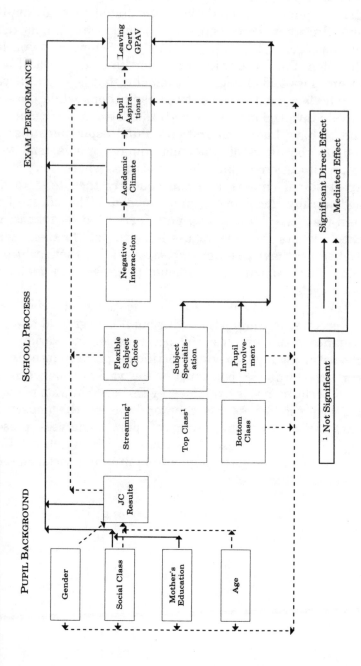

5.11 STABILITY OF SCHOOL EFFECTS

5.11.1 Stability over time

Examination data were collected for the sampled schools in 1996. Due to closures, amalgamations and the expansion of Transition Year provision, Leaving Cert data were available for only 101 schools. There is a high correlation (r = 0.86) between Leaving Cert performance at school level in the two years, that is, schools with higher average performance in 1994 tend to have higher performance in 1996. For English and Maths, the correlations are 0.81 and 0.78 respectively.

When schools are ranked according to their Leaving Cert performance in 1994, 6 of the "top 10" were still in the same position in 1996 while 5 of the "bottom 10" remained in the same group. This indicates greater movement in the ranking of schools for Leaving Cert groups than for their Junior Cert counterparts. However, it should be noted that the massive expansion of Transition Year provision over the year 1995/6 means that the 1996 Leaving Cert group may not fully represent the typical picture in all second-level schools.

TABLE 5.5: REGRESSION OF SCHOOLS' LEAVING CERT GPAV IN 1994 AND 1996 ON PUPIL COMPOSITION

Explanatory variables	*1994*	*1996*
Intercept	4.354	6.847
School type:		
Boys' school	.259	.329
Girls' school	.322	.446
Pupil composition:		
Average social class	-1.025***	-1.051**
Average Junior Cert GPAV	.978***	.706**
Average unemployment	-1.257	-3.106
R^2	0.627	0.535

Note: *** p <.001; ** p <.01

Average Leaving Cert performance in 1994 is significantly related to the social class and ability mix of the school. Overall, pupil composition (gender, class, parental unemployment and Junior Cert performance) explains 63 per cent of the variance between schools in Leaving Cert results (Table 5.5). Pupil performance in

1996 was regressed on pupil composition in 1994. Pupil composition (in 1994) is found to explain 54 per cent of the variance in performance in 1996. School residuals in 1994 are correlated with those in 1996 (r = 0.69) indicating relatively high stability of school effects, controlling for pupil composition.

5.11.2 Stability across school year groups

Stability across school year groups can be assessed by comparing Junior and Leaving Cert groups for 1994 and 1996. In schools where pupils tend to do well in the Junior Cert, pupils tend to do well in the Leaving Cert (r = 0.75 in 1994 and r = 0.76 in 1996). However, the performance of Junior Cert groups within the same school but in different years is more closely related than that of Junior and Leaving Cert groups within the same school in the same year. This may indicate that the treatment of Junior and Leaving Cert groups differs within the same school (through differential use of streaming and curricular packaging) but that the treatment of Junior Cert pupils over time does not vary as much. The relationship between Junior and Leaving Cert performance will be explored in greater detail in Chapter 10. For English, the correlations between Junior and Leaving Cert performance are 0.67 for 1994 and 0.76 for 1996. For Maths, the correlations are 0.73 for 1994 and 0.70 for 1996.

Pupil composition tends to be broadly similar for Junior and Leaving Cert cohorts within the same school, with correlations of 0.87 for parental social class and 0.71 for parental unemployment.[3]

5.12 CONCLUSIONS

The factors influencing senior cycle progress are broadly similar to those shaping performance at the Junior Certificate. Being in a bottom/remedial class has a substantial negative impact on pupil progress over the senior cycle. Pupils tend to do better where they are involved in the school (formally and informally) and where the approach to subject choice is more flexible. The quality of interaction with teachers and the level of teacher expectations continue

---

[3] Some differences in composition would be expected due to the proportion of pupils who drop out of school before the Leaving Certificate.

to play an important role in shaping academic progress among Leaving Certificate pupils.

Differences between Junior and Leaving Cert patterns arise in relation to the effects of disciplinary climate and subject speciali-sation. The effect of disciplinary climate appears to operate indirectly through Junior Cert performance rather than directly on senior cycle progress. In the case of subject specialisation, the degree to which schools can specialise in subjects for the junior cycle is greatly reduced and there is likely to be less potential for synergy between subjects (e.g. pupils can take only one science subject compared with three at Leaving Cert level). The relation-ship between Junior and Leaving Cert performance and progress will be discussed in greater detail in Chapter 10.

Appendix

TABLE A5.1: ALLOCATION OF POINTS TO LEAVING CERTIFICATE
SUBJECT GRADES

Grade	Higher level	Ordinary level
A1	20	12
A2	18	10
B1	17	9
B2	16	8
B3	15	7
C1	14	6
C2	13	5
C3	12	4
D1	11	3
D2	10	2
D3	9	1
Other	0	0

TABLE A5.2: ALLOCATION OF SCORES TO JUNIOR AND INTERMEDIATE
CERTIFICATE SUBJECTS

Grade	Higher	Ordinary	Foundation	Common
A	10	7	4	8
B	9	6	3	7
C	8	5	2	6
D	7	4	1	5
Other	0	0	0	0

TABLE A5.3: EXPLANATORY VARIABLES FOR LEAVING CERTIFICATE
GRADE POINT AVERAGE

Variables	*Description*
Pupil Background	
Gender	Dummy variable where 1= Girl.
Social class	Census Social Class scale ranging from 0 (Higher Professional) to 5 (Unskilled manual worker) based on the occupational status of parents.
Social class unknown	Dummy variable where 1= Social class not reported.
Mother's education	Highest level of mother's education ranging from 0 (primary education) to 4 (university degree).
Parental education unknown	Dummy variable where 1= Mother's/father's education not reported.
Aged 18 and over	Dummy variable where 1= Aged 18 and over on 1st January 1994.
Performance	
Junior/Inter Certificate GPAV	Grade point average in Junior/Inter Cert scored as in Table A5.2; centred on its mean value.
JC results unknown	Dummy variable where 1= Junior/Inter Cert results not reported.
Intermediate Certificate	Dummy variable where 1 = sat Inter rather than Junior Cert.
Repeating Leaving Certificate	Dummy variable where 1= repeating Leaving Certificate.
School social context	
Average social class	Average social class of pupils within the school; centred on its mean value.

School organisation	
Streaming	Extent of streaming and associated curricular differentiation in the school; Guttman scale ranging from 0 (mixed ability base classes) to 4 (highly streamed).
Top class Middle class Bottom class	Set of dummy variables where 1= in top, middle or bottom/remedial class respectively; contrasted against membership of mixed ability base classes.
Involvement	
Formal pupil involvement	Dummy variable where 1= some formal involvement by pupils in the school.
Informal pupil involvement	School-level average of pupil involvement in sports and other extra-curricular activities; centred on mean value.
Curriculum	
Flexible subject choice	Timing of subject choice; ranges from 0 (no choice) to 3 (subject choices made later).
Subject specialisation	Degree of specialisation in the provision of particular subject groupings (see Hannan, Breen et al., 1983).
School Interaction	
Average negative interaction	School-level average of negative teacher interaction; centred on mean.
Academic climate	
Average teacher expectations	School-level average of the highest qualification which teachers expect the pupil to get. Ranges from 1 (Junior Cert) to 4 (University Degree); centred on mean value.
Teacher expectations (individual pupil report)	Highest qualifications which teacher(s) expect the pupil to get; ranges from 0 (Junior Cert) to 3 (university degree).
Educational aspirations	Highest qualifications which the pupil expects to get; ranges from 0 (Junior Cert) to 3 (university degree).

TABLE A5.4: MULTI-LEVEL MODELS OF LEAVING CERTIFICATE GPAV (SCHOOL PROCESS)

	Model					
Fixed effects	*1*	*2*	*3*	*4*	*5*	*6*
Intercept	7.945	7.784	6.970	6.993	7.205	4.105
Pupil background:						
Gender (female)	.199*	.192*	.197*	.179*	.163*	.114
Social class	-.119*	-.115*	-.115*	-.116*	-.110*	-.064*
Social class unknown	-.320	-.317	-.312	-.311	-.292	-.181
Mother's education	.158*	.153*	.151*	.151*	.144*	.092*
Parental education unknown	-1.092*	-1.098*	-1.105*	-1.104*	-1.108*	-.927*
Aged 18 and over	.185	.191	.191	.190	.189	.131
Prior Performance:						
Junior Cert GPAV	2.008*	2.007*	2.008*	2.008*	1.994*	1.601*
JC GPAV unknown	-2.188*	-2.197*	-2.202*	-2.207*	-2.184*	-1.688*
Intermediate Cert	1.651*	1.610*	1.582*	1.573*	1.547*	1.310*
Repeating Leaving Cert	1.569*	1.582*	1.593*	1.595*	1.606*	1.311*
School organisation:						
Streaming	.032	.019	.023	.023	.053	.003
Top class	-.164	-.166	-.147	-.084	-.009	.089
Middle class	-.621	-.624	-.601	-.544	-.515	-.394
Bottom/remedial class	-.891*	-.898*	-.876*	-.814*	-.775*	-.401
Involvement:						
Pupils — formal		.257	.296	.278	.089	.064
Pupils — informal		.612*	.640*	.650*	.486*	.448*
Curriculum:						
Flexible subject choice			.238*	.261*	.210*	.151
Subject specialisation			.142*	.132*	.128*	.100**
School Interaction:						
Average negative interaction				-1.082	-.644	-.678
Academic climate:						
Average teachers' expectations					1.020*	.526*
Teacher expectations[1]						.817*
Pupil aspirations[1]						.711*
Random effects:						
School-level variance	0.686*	0.630*	0.580*	0.556*	0.475*	0.383*
Pupil-level variance	5.405*	5.404*	5.403*	5.404*	5.405*	4.771*
Deviance	21539.6	21530.9	21522.9	21520.0	21507.1	20911.3
Degrees of freedom	14	16	18	19	20	24
Improvement in deviance[2]	<.001	<.05	<.05	<.10	<.001	<.001

Note: * $p < .05$;

[1] Dummy variables for missing information on these variables were included in the analysis but are not reported here.

[2] For model 1, this represents improvement over the null model (Model 1, Table 5.2). For the other models, the comparison is with the previous model.

Chapter 6

SCHOOL ATTENDANCE AND PUPIL DROP-OUT

School attendance and drop-out must be considered as important outcomes of the educational process. British research has indicated that not only does truancy have a negative effect on exam results but that it is strongly associated with poor outcomes in education, training and the labour market in the period following schooling (Casey and Smith, 1995). It is evident that pupils will receive fewer benefits from the educational process if they are persistently absent from school; the influence of absenteeism rates on pupil performance in the Junior Certificate examination will be assessed in Chapter 9. Irish research has indicated that young people who leave school before the end of the senior cycle are less likely to obtain employment and have limited access to further education/training (Smyth, Hannan, 1995; McCoy, Whelan, 1996). Schools have been found to vary significantly in their drop-out rates (see Cheng, 1995, on British schools). Therefore, it is important to take account of those who leave school early as well as those who sit the Leaving Certificate when considering the influence of schools on their pupils.

6.1 SCHOOL ATTENDANCE

Information was collected from schools about the attendance records of Junior Certificate pupils over the past year. Pupils were categorised by teachers as having "good" (>90%), "average" (80-90%) or "poor" (<80%) attendance records. This classification can be externally validated by examining the proportion of pupils who were absent from school on the day of the ability tests. It was found that 5 per cent of those classified as good attenders were absent from school on that day compared with 16 per cent of average attenders and 34 per cent of poor attenders. Therefore, the measure of attendance provides a good indicator of actual pupil behaviour, although it would have been preferable to have more detailed information on the exact level of school absence.

TABLE 6.1: SCHOOL ATTENDANCE BY SCHOOL SECTOR AND GENDER

	Secondary							
	Boys'	Girls'	Coed		Vocational		Community/ Comprehensive	
			Boys	Girls	Boys	Girls	Boys	Girls
Good	83.2	78.7	80.1	79.6	67.3	70.5	77.4	70.4
Average	12.6	15.8	15.3	18.0	21.1	15.3	14.6	18.6
Poor	4.2	5.5	4.6	2.5	11.6	14.2	8.0	7.0
N	934	1,312	437	518	757	490	279	246

Table 6.1 indicates that the majority of pupils have good attendance records. However, school attendance varies according to
school sector. Poor attendance is more prevalent among pupils in
vocational schools and lowest among those in secondary schools.
These school types also differ in terms of pupil composition (see
Chapter 4), however, and these compositional differences must be
taken into account when assessing the impact of school sector on
pupil attendance. The following sections will assess the impact of
pupil characteristics on absenteeism levels, and allow us to
explore the extent to which school characteristics shape patterns
of non-attendance. For the purposes of this analysis, those with
"poor" and "average" attendance records are grouped together and
referred to as the "high absenteeism" group. Using this grouping,
individual schools are found to differ significantly in the proportion of their pupils who have high absenteeism records, varying
from none to 57 per cent of the Junior Certificate cohort.

FIGURE 6.1: "RAW" SCHOOL DIFFERENCES IN HIGH ABSENTEEISM

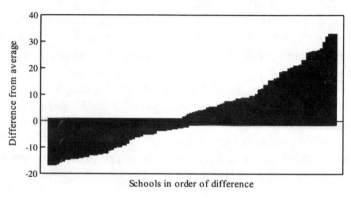

Schools in order of difference

A multi-level logit model was used to assess the impact of pupil and school characteristics on high absenteeism; the results of this analysis are presented in Table 6.2 with explanatory variables described in Table A6.1. The coefficients indicate the impact of particular factors on the log odds of having a high absenteeism rate. The baseline model indicates that there is a significant difference between schools in the proportion of pupils who have high absenteeism rates (Model 1, Table 6.2).[1] Figure 6.1 illustrates the extent of this variation, showing the difference between the predicted probability of high absenteeism for each school compared with the average absenteeism level across all schools; the predicted probability of high absenteeism ranges from 3 per cent to 51 per cent.

6.1.1 Pupil background

Model 2 (Table 6.2) indicates the impact of social background on absenteeism levels. Girls have a slightly lower absenteeism rate than boys, although the difference is not statistically significant. Parental social class has a strong and significant impact on high absenteeism; the odds of absenteeism among those from an unskilled manual background are almost twice (1.9 times) as high as among those from a higher professional background. The "social class unknown" group also has a higher absenteeism rate than those from professional backgrounds; this group may include pupils whose parents are long-term unemployed and therefore have no identifiable occupational category to report. In addition to social class, mother's education has a strong effect on absenteeism rates; pupils whose mothers went to university have only 0.7 times the level of absenteeism of those with only a primary education, even controlling for social class. Those who are older than average (aged 16 or over) tend to have significantly higher absenteeism rates than their younger counterparts.

Pupils with higher verbal and numerical ability test scores have significantly lower absenteeism rates than those with lower test scores (Model 3, Table 6.2). The direction of influence in this case is likely to be complex; lower ability pupils may exhibit a long history of absenteeism, perhaps dating back to primary school, which in turn widens the gap in performance between them and their higher ability counterparts. The "missing for ability test"

---

[1] Because the outcome variable is a binary response, variation among pupils within schools is not estimated.

term takes account of the fact that persistent absentees were unlikely to be in school on the day of ability testing, but takes
account of their other characteristics when assessing the processes shaping school attendance. The effects of social class and
mother's education are reduced slightly but remain significant
when ability is taken into account. Gender becomes significant,
indicating that boys are more likely to be absent from school than
girls of the same ability level.

6.1.2 School social context

Model 4 (Table 6.2) takes account of the school social context, that
is, the class composition of pupils within a school. The social class
context is found to have a significant effect on absenteeism, with
higher levels found in predominantly working-class schools. Figure 6.2 indicates the predicted probability of high absenteeism in
each of the schools, centred on the average rate across all schools,
controlling for pupil background, ability and social context. Even
taking pupil composition factors into account, significant
differences remain between schools in their absenteeism levels.

FIGURE 6.2: ADJUSTED SCHOOL DIFFERENCES IN ABSENTEEISM

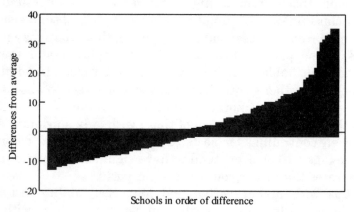

Schools in order of difference

6.1.3 School type

There are no significant differences in absenteeism levels between
secondary, vocational and community/comprehensive schools once
we take into account the nature of pupil intake to each school type
(Model 5, Table 6.2). Therefore, the higher absenteeism found
among pupils in vocational schools (see Table 6.1) is due to the

over-representation of lower ability and working-class pupils in this sector rather than to sectoral effects *per se*.

TABLE 6.2: MULTI-LEVEL MODELS OF HIGH ABSENTEEISM AMONG JUNIOR CERTIFICATE PUPILS (N=4,973)

	Model					
Fixed effects	*1*	*2*	*3*	*4*	*5*	*6*
Intercept	-1.485*	-1.531*	-1.700*	-1.724*	-1.836*	-1.388*
Pupil background:						
Gender (female)		-.131	-.196*	-.193*	.052	.083
Social class		.128*	.080*	.067*	.069*	.045
Social class unknown		.976*	.708*	.666*	.674*	.572*
Mother's education[1]		-.180*	-.141*	-.132*	-.133*	-.095*
Aged 16 and over		.562*	.302*	.293*	.293*	.235
Ability:						
VRNA score			-.028*	-.027*	-.027*	-.016*
Missing for ability test			1.700*	1.700*	1.715*	1.601*
School context:						
Average social class				.456*	.502*	
School type:						
Coed Secondary Coed					.141	
Secondary* Girls					-.098	
Vocational					.122	
Vocational* Girls					-.522	
Comm./Comp.					-.254	
Comm./Comp.* Girls					.012	
Teacher-pupil interaction:						
Positive interaction[1]						-.226*
Negative interaction[1]						.473*
Academic climate:						
Average teachers' expectations						-.691*
Teachers' expectations[1]						-.188*
Pupil aspirations[1]						-.301*
Random effects School-level variance	0.862*	0.703*	0.727*	0.685*	0.678*	0.709*

Note: * p<.05.

   [1] Dummy variables for missing information on these variables were included in the analysis but are not reported here.

6.1.4 School organisation and process

The social context of a school is found to have a significant impact on pupil absenteeism levels. However, average social class is highly correlated with many aspects of school organisation and process. In order to "unpack" the effects of schools on pupil attendance, average social class and school type were removed from the model and other aspects of school organisation were investigated.

Model 6 (Table 6.2) presents the final model for pupil absenteeism. Only significant school-level variables are included in the model. However, it is also worth reporting the non-significant effects. Research in Britain (see Casey and Smith, 1995) had indicated that school resources, such as the pupil-teacher ratio, have a significant impact on truancy levels among second-level pupils. However, the Irish data indicate no significant impact of full-time (or part-time) pupil-teacher ratio on high absenteeism. Aspects of school management, including the frequency and importance of staff meetings, were found to have no significant impact on absenteeism rates.

Streaming and the nature of class allocation within streamed schools have been hypothesised to increase overall levels of absenteeism due to the lower attachment to school found among pupils in bottom classes (see Bryk and Thum, 1989). While preliminary analysis indicates a higher absenteeism rate among those in bottom classes within the current sample, this effect is not apparent once pupil background and ability are taken into account.

Absenteeism rates might be expected to be lower where pupils and parents experience greater involvement in the school. Absenteeism is indeed found to be lower where there is a higher level of informal involvement among pupils, though this difference is not significant once intake is controlled for. Formal pupil involvement, such as the existence of a pupils' council, has no significant impact on school attendance. Furthermore, absenteeism tends to be somewhat lower where there is an active parents' association and/or high levels of attendance at parent-teacher meetings. However, these relationships are not statistically significant once we take into account the mix of pupils attending a school.

In contrast, the nature of interaction between teachers and pupils has a highly significant effect on pupil absenteeism. Pupils are more likely to be absent from school when they report negative interaction with teachers, and are less likely to be absent when they experience more positive interaction. The average level of positive or negative teacher interaction in a school does not have a significant impact, however. This would seem to indicate significant variation in the individual experiences of pupils within schools in relation to interaction with teachers.

The academic orientation of the school has a significant impact on absenteeism levels. Absenteeism levels are significantly lower where teachers in a school have high expectations for pupils regarding their level of education. This is an aggregate effect which operates over and above the pupil's own expectations and her/his perceptions of teacher expectations. Pupils tend to have lower absenteeism levels where they themselves expect to go on to the Leaving Certificate and further/higher education. Pupil aspirations mediate the effects of gender, parental social class and age, indicating that girls, middle class pupils and those of average age have lower absenteeism rates because they tend to have higher educational aspirations.

Even controlling for pupil-teacher interaction and academic orientation, significant differences exist between schools in their absenteeism levels. It is likely that more detailed information on the disciplinary climate and specific policy towards absenteeism within a school would yield greater insights. This issue will be explored in the case-studies of schools (see Chapter 11).

6.2 PUPIL DROP-OUT

Three measures of pupil drop-out were compiled: potential drop-out, which is based on pupils' reported intentions to leave school after the Junior Certificate; junior cycle drop-out, based on school records regarding enrolment figures; and senior cycle drop-out, based on school enrolment records.

6.2.1 Potential drop-out

Junior Certificate pupils were questioned about their plans after the Junior Cert exam. Table 6.3 indicates that the majority of pupils have definite intentions to stay at school to take the Leaving Certificate. A minority report definite intentions to leave school: to look for a job, enter an apprenticeship or take part in a vocational training course. A slightly larger group report that they will "probably" (but not definitely) stay on to the Leaving Certificate. For the purposes of the following analysis, all of those who are not definite about staying on for the Leaving Cert are grouped together. While some of this group may go on to complete the

Do Schools Differ?

senior cycle, they exhibit weaker attachment to school and are likely to be at much greater risk of dropping-out than their "definite" counterparts. Table 6.3 indicates that potential drop-out varies by gender and school sector. Girls are much more likely than boys to report definite intentions to complete the senior cycle, a pattern that is evident within all types of schools[2]. Those in vocational schools, both boys and girls, report higher potential drop-out than those in other sectors.

TABLE 6.3: POTENTIAL DROP-OUT BY SCHOOL SECTOR AND GENDER

	Secondary						Community/ Comprehensive	
	Boys'	Girls'	Coed		Vocational		sive	
			Boys	Girls	Boys	Girls	Boys	Girls
Definitely stay	79.1	86.2	73.1	89.7	51.8	69.7	67.7	85.1
Probably stay	14.8	10.7	15.1	8.3	25.0	20.1	15.8	10.7
Definitely leave:								
Job/apprenticeship	3.9	1.2	5.7	1.2	14.9	6.0	8.9	2.1
Vocational training	2.2	1.9	6.0	0.8	8.3	4.2	7.6	2.1
N	1,002	1,370	448	536	757	508	662	568

Table 6.4 presents a series of multi-level models assessing the impact of pupil and school characteristics on the log odds of intending to drop out from school. Model 1 indicates that there is substantial variation between schools in terms of potential drop-out, a pattern which is represented graphically in Figure 6.3. The predicted probabilities of drop-out across all second-level schools range from 6 per cent to 58 per cent.

---

[2] A gender difference in actual drop-out rates is evident from national surveys of school leavers (see McCoy, Whelan, 1996).

FIGURE 6.3: "RAW" SCHOOL DIFFERENCES IN POTENTIAL DROP-OUT

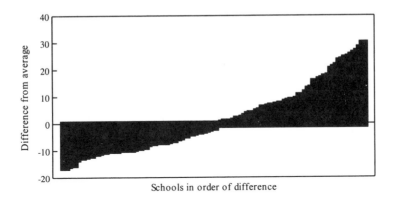

6.2.2 Pupil background

Girls have significantly lower potential drop-out rates than boys, controlling for social background and age (Model 2, Table 6.4). Working-class pupils are more likely to report that they may leave school after the Junior Certificate; those from unskilled manual backgrounds are more than twice as likely as those from a higher professional background to report such intentions. Similarly, the "social class unknown" group is significantly more likely to be at risk of drop-out than middle-class pupils. Maternal education also has a significant effect on drop-out, over and above that of social background; pupils whose mothers have higher levels of education are less likely to intend to drop-out. Older pupils (aged 16 and over) are more likely to report intending to drop-out. This group includes those who have been "kept back" over the junior cycle or in primary school. Their "at risk" status would appear to reflect a more negative experience of schools (see section on absenteeism); in addition, this group are more likely to be legally able to leave school at an earlier time-point.

Higher ability pupils are less likely to report intending to leave school early (Model 3, Table 6.4). Some of the effects of social class, maternal education and age are mediated through pupil ability, although these variables remain significant when ability is taken into account.

TABLE 6.4: MULTI-LEVEL MODELS OF POTENTIAL DROP-OUT AMONG JUNIOR CERT PUPILS (N=4,888)

Fixed effects	Model						
	1	2	3	4	5	6	7
Intercept	-1.329*	-1.001*	-1.096*	-1.085*	-1.304*	-.711*	-.902*
Pupil background:							
Gender (female)		-.968*	-1.099*	-1.096*	-.859*	-.887*	-.887*
Social class		.153*	.073*	.041	.041	.049	.031
Social class unknown		1.014*	.515*	.404*	.424*	.297	.175
Mother's education[1]		-.257*	-.208*	-.188*	-.193*	-.195*	-.177*
Aged 16 and over		.938*	.584*	.573*	.554*	.578*	.530*
Ability:							
VRNA score			-.053*	-.052*	-.051*	-.046*	-.043*
Missing for ability test			1.010*	1.000*	1.000*	.909*	.656*
School context:							
Average social class				.433*	.276*		
School type:							
Coed Secondary					.228		
Coed Secondary* Girls					-.442		
Vocational					.503*		
Vocational* Girls					-.150		
Comm./Comp.					.060		
Comm./Comp.* Girls					-.338		
School organisation:							
Streaming						.037	.017
Bottom/remedial class						.491*	.513*
School management:							
Importance of staff meetings[1]						-.150	-.170
Staff council						-.267	-.319*
Involvement:							
Pupils-formal						-.166	-.120
Pupils-informal						-.259	-.141
Parents-subject choice						-.118	-.035
School Interaction:							
Strict school						-.222*	-.120
Positive interaction[1]						-.645*	-.612*
Negative interaction[1]						.577*	.512*
Mediating variables:							
Average teachers' expectations							-.619*
High absenteeism							.743*
Part-time work							.172
Random effects							
School-level variance	0.623*	0.293*	0.186*	0.142*	0.108*	0.170*	0.120*

Note: * p<.05.

[1] Dummy variables for missing information on these variables were included in the analysis but are not reported here.

6.2.3 School social context

The social class context of a school has a significant impact on potential drop-out, with higher rates reported in predominantly working-class than in middle-class schools (Model 4, Table 6.4). Individual social class background is no longer significant in this model, indicating that the effects of parental class on potential drop-out are mediated through the social class context of the school. Even controlling for school composition, however, significant differences remain between schools in potential drop-out levels (see Figure 6.4).

FIGURE 6.4: ADJUSTED SCHOOL DIFFERENCES IN POTENTIAL DROP-OUT

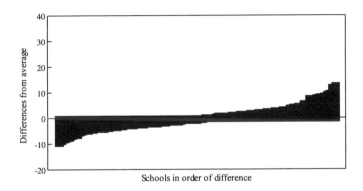

6.2.4 School type

School type has a significant impact on drop-out, with pupils in vocational schools more likely to report intending to leave school early than those in other school types. This effect operates over and above the impact of differences in pupil composition between the school sectors (see Model 5, Table 6.4).

6.2.5 School organisation and process

The impact of school characteristics on drop-out intentions is represented in Model 6. It is worth noting that other factors, such as school size or pupil-teacher ratio, have no appreciable effect on potential drop-out and are thus excluded from this model. In general, a relatively small number of significant effects can be identified. School organisation has a significant impact with higher potential drop-out found in streamed schools. However, this effect is accounted for by the higher reported drop-out among those in bottom or remedial classes with no such disadvantage for pupils in top or middle classes (Model 6, Table 6.4).

There is some evidence that pupil drop-out is less likely where there is a more inclusive atmosphere within the school, that is, where pupils, parents and teachers are more directly involved in the schooling structure. Thus, the nature of school management has some impact on potential drop-out, with lower rates where staff meetings are considered important by the school principal and/or where a staff council exists. These effects are below statistical significance, however. The nature of pupil involvement has some effect, with an association between higher levels of formal and informal involvement and lower rates of reported drop-out (Model 6, Table 6.4). Drop-out is also somewhat lower where parents are actively involved in subject choice for pupils, although involvement in parent-teacher meetings or parents' associations does not appear to have an appreciable effect.

Levels of intended drop-out are lower where pupils tend to perceive the school as strict (Model 6, Table 6.4). Pupils who report positive interaction with their teachers are less likely to intend to leave school early while the opposite is the case for those who report negative interaction. These effects do not operate at an aggregate level, however, indicating the importance of looking at variation within schools in pupils' experiences of education. In overall terms, therefore, pupils are less likely to leave school early where they experience the school environment as "strict but fair".

Model 7 (Table 6.4) reports the effects of mediating variables on pupil drop-out. Pupils are less likely to intend to leave school early where schools have a positive academic climate, that is, where teachers expect most pupils to stay on in full-time education. The effect of strictness and parental and pupil involvement are reduced somewhat in this model, indicating that these features are associated with the academic climate of the school. Pupils who have poor attendance records are more likely to intend to leave school early; the odds of those with high absenteeism levels intending to leave are more than twice those of pupils with average/good attendance records. In addition, those who have part-time jobs have a slight but non-significant tendency to report drop-out intentions; a much stronger association between part-time work and early school leaving has been found in the British and American contexts (Dustmann *et al.*, 1996; McNeal, 1997; Eckstein and Wolpin, 1998). This pattern may reflect the relative scarcity of unskilled "youth jobs" on a full-time basis in the Irish labour market at the time of the survey.

The above characteristics do not account for the differences between sectors in drop-out rates, with pupils in vocational schools more likely to intend to drop-out, even taking into account differences in school management, parental and pupil involvement, teacher interaction and expectations, and pupil attendance. It is difficult to account for this difference. It may be that there are some unmeasured differences between pupils in vocational schools and those in other school types; for example, parents who do not expect their children to stay on in full-time education may be more likely to send their children to a vocational school.

6.3 ACTUAL DROP-OUT RATES

The previous section described potential drop-out rates among Junior Certificate pupils. Information was also collected from school principals on actual drop-out rates over the junior and senior cycle (see Figure 6.5). As might be expected, second-level schools tend to have a higher drop-out rate over the senior than the junior cycle. At the junior cycle, over one-third of schools experience no overall drop-out; the highest drop-out rate is 41 per cent, with schools averaging 4.5 per cent. At senior cycle, one-quarter of schools experience no drop-out; the highest drop-out rate is 69 per cent, with an average of 15 per cent over all schools. Drop-out rates are significantly correlated at the school level ($r = 0.3$); that is, schools with high junior cycle drop-out tend to experience relatively high senior cycle drop-out.

FIGURE 6.5: JUNIOR AND SENIOR CYCLE DROP-OUT RATES

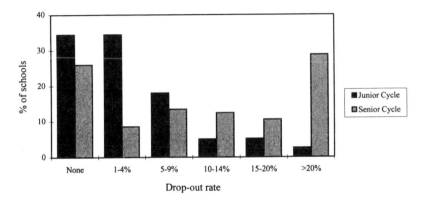

Table 6.5 indicates that the level of drop-out varies significantly by school sector. Vocational schools report the highest actual drop-out at both levels with the lowest rate found within the secondary sector, particularly coed secondary schools.

TABLE 6.5: ACTUAL DROP-OUT RATES BY SCHOOL SECTOR

	Secondary				
	Boys'	*Girls'*	*Coed*	*Vocational*	*Community/ Comprehensive*
Junior Cycle	2.9%	3.9%	3.2%	7.1%	3.8%
Senior Cycle	12.1%	13.0%	6.0%	21.1%	17.2%

The analyses of potential drop-out separated out the effect of schooling factors from pupil-level characteristics. In contrast, aggregate school-level data are used to examine actual drop-out rates and, consequently, no information is available on the characteristics of the pupils who have already dropped out of second-level schools. However, it is possible to examine the differences between schools with low drop-out and those with high drop-out levels.

Table 6.6 indicates that the factors associated with actual drop-out rates are broadly similar to those associated with potential drop-out. Pupil drop-out is strongly associated with pupil composition factors; drop-out is higher in schools where pupils come from predominantly working-class backgrounds and have parents with lower levels of education. Drop-out is also strongly related to the ability mix of the school with higher drop-out where pupils are of lower ability. At Junior Certificate level, having a somewhat older group of pupils is associated with higher drop-out.

Highly streamed schools have greater drop-out over the senior cycle. At junior cycle level, streamed schools have somewhat higher drop-out rates but the effect is not statistically significant. Schools tend to have lower pupil drop-out when pupils are formally integrated into the school through pupils' councils or prefect systems and where parents are more involved in subject choice. The ethos of the school also has an impact with greater drop-out in schools that are seen as "easy-going" and "friendly" rather than "strict" by pupils. However, contrary to what might be expected, drop-out rates are higher in more "organised"

TABLE 6.6: CHARACTERISTICS OF HIGH DROP-OUT SCHOOLS

	Junior Cycle (>5%)	*Senior cycle (>20%)*
Pupil composition	Older pupils Working class*** Lower parental education* Lower ability*	Working class*** Lower parental education*** Lower ability*
School organisation		Streamed school*
Disciplinary climate	Less strict/more easy-going school More organised school More friendly school High absenteeism rate*	Less strict school
Involvement		Less formal pupil involvement* Less parental involvement in subject choice
Academic climate	Low teacher expectations*** Low pupil expectations***	Low teacher expectations*** Low pupil expectations Lower average study hours

Note: *p<.05,***p<.001

schools. At junior cycle level, higher drop-out is associated with higher rates of absenteeism in the school as a whole. In addition, school drop-out is higher where schools have a less positive academic climate, as indicated by teacher expectations, pupil aspirations and, at senior cycle, time spent on homework/study. It should be noted that much of this information (e.g., pupil aspirations, homework/study time) has been collected from pupils four to five months before their formal examinations. Pupils who have already dropped out of school by this time are likely to have had even lower aspirations and commitment to school and thus the information may underestimate the overall effects of pupil composition and school characteristics.

6.4 CONCLUSIONS

This chapter has outlined some of the key aspects of the schooling process which influence school attendance and pupil drop-out. The findings indicate that working-class pupils and pupils in predominantly working-class schools have a higher absenteeism rate and remain at greater risk of dropping out of full-time second-level education (see also Smyth, Hannan, 1995). In addition, girls are more likely to intend to stay on in school than boys. Absenteeism rates are found to be higher among potential early leavers, a pattern which may facilitate the targeting of "at risk" pupils for intervention at the school and local level. The relationship between absenteeism, drop-out and academic performance will be discussed in greater detail in Chapter 9.

Schools differ significantly in absenteeism and drop-out rates, over and above the effects of pupil background. Many of the same factors shape the two outcomes. In particular, a positive academic climate within the school promotes higher attendance rates and retention within the schooling system. Absenteeism levels and drop-out rates are higher where pupils have had a negative experience of interaction with teachers and lower where interaction has been positive. Potential drop-out is higher in bottom classes within streamed schools; thus, this group of pupils are less likely to remain within the schooling system and underperform academically when they do remain in school (see Chapters 4 and 5). In addition, an inclusive school atmosphere with greater staff, pupil and parental involvement helps to retain pupils within full-time education.

The pattern of differentiation by school sector indicates that drop-out rates are higher within vocational schools, a pattern that is not explicable in terms of differences in pupil composition. These differences persist when account is taken of streaming, school involvement and interaction, and academic climate. This pattern is difficult to explain but may relate to different historical traditions in each of the schooling sectors. It should be noted, however, that there is considerable variation among vocational schools in their pupil drop-out rates.

Appendix

APPENDIX TABLE A6.1: EXPLANATORY VARIABLES IN RELATION TO ABSENTEEISM AND PUPIL DROP-OUT

Variables	Description
Pupil Background	
Gender	Dummy variable where 1= Girl.
Social class	Census Social Class scale ranging from 0 (Higher Professional) to 5 (Unskilled manual worker) based on the occupational status of parents.
Mother's education	Highest level of mother's education ranging from 0 (primary education) to 4 (university degree).
Aged 16 and over	Dummy variable where 1= Aged 16 or over on 1st January 1994.
Ability	
Ability	VRNA, combined verbal reasoning and numerical ability scores; centred on its mean value.
Missing for ability test	Dummy variable where 1= Absent from school on day of VRNA test.
School social context	
Average social class	Average social class of pupils within the school; centred on its mean value.
School management	
Importance of staff meetings	Principal's rating of importance of staff meetings; ranges from 0 (not important) to 2 (very important).
Staff council	Dummy variable where 1= staff council in school.
School organisation	
Streaming	Extent of streaming and associated curricular differentiation in the school; Guttman scale ranging from 0 (mixed ability classes) to 4 (highly streamed).
Bottom class	Dummy variable where 1= in bottom/remedial class.

Involvement	
Formal pupil involvement	Dummy variable where 1= some formal involvement by pupils in the school.
Informal pupil involvement	School-level average of pupil involvement in sports and other extra-curricular activities; centred on mean value.
Parental involvement in subject choice	School-level involvement of parents in pupils' choice of subjects; ranges from 0 (none) to 2 (high).
Disciplinary climate	
Strict school	School-level average of pupil rating of school as "strict" – "easy-going"; centred on mean value.
School Interaction	
Friendly school	School-level average of pupil rating of school as "unfriendly" – "friendly"; centred on mean value.
Organised school	School-level average of pupil rating of school as "organised" – "disorganised"; centred on mean value.
Positive teacher interaction	Likert scale based on frequency of following items: (1) Have you been told that your work is good? (2) Have you been asked questions in class? (3) Have you been praised for answering a difficult question correctly? (4) Have you been praised because your written work is well done? Reliability: alpha is 0.68 (JC) and 0.67 (LC). Ranges from 0 (low) to 3 (high).
Negative teacher interaction	Likert scale based on frequency of following items: (1) Have you been given out to because your work is untidy or not done on time? (2) Have you wanted to ask or answer questions in class but were ignored? (3) Have you been given out to for misbehaving in class? (4) Teachers pay more attention in class to what some pupils say than to others. (5) I find most teachers hard to talk to. Reliability: alpha is 0.59 (JC) and 0.61 (LC). Values range from 0 (low) to 3 (high).

Academic climate	
Average hours of study	School-level average of no. of hours of study/homework per night; centred on average value.
Average teacher expectations	School-level average of the highest qualification which teachers expect the pupil to get. Ranges from 1 (Junior Cert) to 4 (University Degree); centred on mean value.
Teacher expectations (individual pupil report)	Highest qualifications which teacher(s) expect the pupil to get; ranges from 0 (Junior Cert) to 3 (university degree).
Educational aspirations	Highest qualifications which the pupil expects to get; ranges from 0 (Junior Cert) to 3 (university degree).
Pupil commitment to school	
High absenteeism	Dummy variable where 1= pupil has poor/average attendance over the previous year.
Part-time work	Dummy variable where 1= pupil held a part-time job at time of interview.

Chapter 7

SCHOOLS AND PERSONAL DEVELOPMENT

Second-level schools are faced with a complex set of goals, attempting to enhance not only the academic development of pupils but also the personal and social development of young people over the crucial period of adolescence. Previous research has indicated that young people have a broadly positive view of how schools have contributed to their personal development (see Hannan, Smyth *et al.*, 1996; Hannan, Ó Riain, 1993). However, it is also apparent that the exam years represent a relatively stressful time for young people (Hannan, Smyth *et al.*, 1996). This chapter focuses on the impact of school organisation and process on current stress levels and aspects of personal/social development among Junior and Leaving Certificate pupils. The concern is with examining the influence of schools, independently of pupil composition factors.

7.1 SCHOOL EFFECTS ON PERSONAL DEVELOPMENT

Table 7.1 indicates the extent of variation among schools in a range of pupil outcomes, both academic and non-academic. The intra-school correlation indicates the amount of variation in a particular outcome which is attributable to the school, before controlling for pupil composition or school characteristics. It is clear that the greatest difference between schools is found in relation to academic performance (see Chapters 4 and 5). In contrast, only two to five per cent of the total variation in pupil development outcomes is attributable to the school level.

This pattern is not altogether surprising. One of the primary purposes of schools is to foster intellectual development among their pupils and examination performance represents a potential, though far from perfect, measure of such development. In contrast, few would argue that the enhancement of body image should represent an explicit objective of the schooling process. Thus, schools are more likely to influence the outcomes on which they focus more explicitly.[1] In addition, personal-social development among pupils is likely to be subject to a very broad range of influences, including family circumstances, neighbourhood effects, peer groups (outside school) and so on. It is not unusual, therefore, that there are considerable differences in pupil development among those in the same school.

TABLE 7.1: SCHOOL VARIATION IN PUPIL OUTCOMES
(INTRA-SCHOOL CORRELATION)

Pupil outcome	Junior Certificate	Leaving Certificate
Exam performance	0.223	0.198
Current stress	0.042	0.055
Academic self-image	0.032	0.029
Locus of control	0.024	0.017
Body image	0.050	0.048

In spite of these seemingly small school effects, however, it is worth exploring whether certain aspects of the schooling process can influence pupil development for better or worse. The remainder of this chapter focuses on assessing these school-level influences.

7.2 CURRENT STRESS

Current stress levels among pupils in the sampled schools were measured using an adapted version of the General Health Questionnaire (GHQ) items (see Hannan, Smyth *et al.*, 1996, for further details). Figure 7.1 indicates that levels of current stress are much higher among Junior and Leaving Certificate pupils than among young adults. A relatively high proportion of pupils, particularly at Leaving Certificate level, report inability to concentrate, losing sleep over worry, and feeling constantly under strain (see Hannan, Smyth *et al.*, 1996). Evidently, exam years are extremely stressful for students, particularly those doing the Leaving Cert. Girls, in particular, report much higher stress levels than boys.

---

[1] It is noteworthy, however, that teachers and school management tend to adopt a complex view of the objectives of schooling (see Chapter 11).

FIGURE 7.1: "FEELING CONSTANTLY UNDER STRAIN" (MORE/MUCH MORE THAN USUAL)

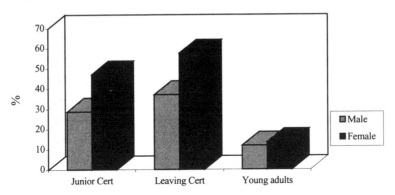

Most (95 per cent) of the variation in stress[2] levels is found among pupils within schools, although schools do vary significantly from each other in their average stress levels. Figure 7.2 illustrates the extent of school-level differences in stress levels among Junior Certificate pupils; the pattern is broadly similar for Leaving Cert pupils.

FIGURE 7.2: "RAW" SCHOOL DIFFERENCES IN JUNIOR CERT STRESS

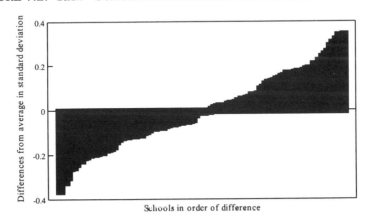

---

[2] The derivation of the stress measure and of the explanatory variables is described in Tables A7.1 and A7.2.

7.2.1 Pupil background

Girls report significantly higher stress levels than boys, even controlling for social background and prior ability/performance. Social class background, mother's education and age of pupil have no significant impact on stress. Current stress is significantly associated with prior ability/performance; pupils with higher ability test or Junior Certificate scores tend to report higher stress levels (Tables A7.3 and A7.4). Stress levels tend to be somewhat lower in predominantly working-class schools, though this effect is significant at the Junior Cert level only. In overall terms, a very high proportion (69-72 per cent) of the initial difference between schools in average stress levels is explained by the gender, class and ability mix of their pupils. Figure 7.3 indicates the substantial reduction in school-level variation when pupil composition is taken into account.

FIGURE 7.3: ADJUSTED SCHOOL DIFFERENCES IN JUNIOR CERT STRESS

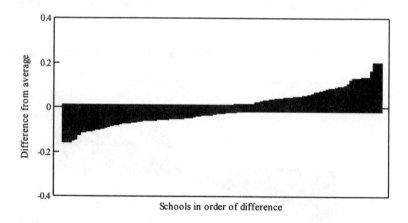

7.2.2 School type

It may appear, then, that schools can have little independent impact on stress levels among their pupils. However, a significant but small difference remains between schools and certain aspects of the schooling process are found to have a significant influence. Stress levels do not vary substantially by the type of school pupils attend, although there is a tendency towards lower stress levels among those in vocational schools, particularly among boys (Table 7.2).

7.2.3 School organisation and process

Curricular packaging influences pupil stress levels within the school. Pupils tend to report higher stress (by 0.145 standard deviations) where they have experienced restricted subject choice within the school (Table 7.2); this may occur because pupils do not see the school as responsive to their particular needs or abilities. At the Junior Cert level, taking fewer exam subjects appears to be associated with lower stress levels (Table 7.2). This pattern is not apparent among Leaving Cert pupils where there is much less variation between pupils in the number of exam subjects taken. Contrary to what might have been expected, stress levels are slightly but significantly higher where parents are actively involved in pupils' choice of subjects. This pattern may reflect greater academic emphasis in such schools.

Having clear homework rules helps to reduce stress levels through giving pupils consistent feedback about their academic progress. Stress levels are also lower where pupils experience positive interaction with, and feedback from, their teachers. Conversely, negative interaction with teachers and with other pupils (a high level of bullying) increases pupil stress levels. In contrast to the clear effects of informal interaction, the existence of a formalised pastoral care programme within the school has no significant impact on reducing pupil stress levels.

Certain aspects of school ethos are associated with reduced stress levels, though the pattern occurs somewhat differently for Junior and Leaving Certificate pupils. At Junior Cert level, schools characterised as friendly by pupils are associated with lower stress, while lower stress is associated with higher school satisfaction at Leaving Cert level. At Leaving Cert level, a strong academic orientation within the school, as indicated by the average number of hours of study/homework done by pupils, is associated with higher stress levels.

In summary, while much of the variation in pupil stress levels is not explained by schooling factors, key aspects of school process can play an important role in enhancing or reducing young people's experience of stress. In particular, the nature of interaction with teachers and other pupils along with the general school climate have significant effects on pupil stress levels. It is worth noting that many of the factors (such as interaction with teachers, bullying, restricted subject choice) affect pupils differently within the same school so that attention should be paid to assessing within-school variation in stress levels.

TABLE 7.2: SCHOOL CHARACTERISTICS AND PUPIL STRESS LEVELS

Fixed effects	Junior Certificate			Leaving Certificate		
	Model			Model		
	1	2	3	1	2	3
School context:						
Average social class	-.097*	-.069*		-.022	.001	
School type:						
Coed Secondary		-.064			-.086	
Coed Secondary* Girls		.062			.058	
Vocational		-.133*			-.128	
Vocational* Girls		.083			.026	
Comm./Comp.		-.110			-.017	
Comm./Comp.* Girls		.186			-.027	
Curriculum:						
Number of subjects (low)			-.113*			-
Restricted subject choice			.145*			.164*
Parental involvement in subject choice			.061*			.050*
Disciplinary climate:						
Homework rules			-.066*			-.052
Interaction:						
Friendly school			-.110*			-
Positive pupil-teacher interaction			-.175*			-.173*
Negative pupil-teacher interaction			.307*			.201*
Level of bullying in the school			.405*			.571*
Average pupil satisfaction			-			-.186*
Academic climate:						
Average hours of study	-	-	-			.108*
Random effects						
School-level variance	0.011*	0.010*	0.006*	0.017*	0.015*	0.013*
Pupil-level variance	0.898*	0.897*	0.847*	0.883*	0.883*	0.812*

Note: * p<.05.

All models are controlled for gender, pupil background and ability. The coefficients for pupil background and ability factors are reported in Tables A7.3 and A7.4.

7.3 ACADEMIC SELF-IMAGE

Academic self-image refers to a pupil's evaluation of his/her academic abilities and competence. The scale is derived from items asking the pupil to rate her/himself relative to other pupils and to teacher demands (see Table A7.1). Figure 7.4 indicates that schools differ significantly from each other in the self-ratings of their pupils. However, most (97 per cent) of the variation in academic self-image is among pupils rather than schools (see Table 7.1).

FIGURE 7.4: "RAW" SCHOOL DIFFERENCES IN ACADEMIC SELF-IMAGE — JUNIOR CERT PUPILS

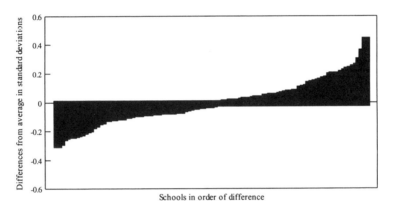

7.3.1 Pupil background

Girls tend to have lower academic self-images than boys (see Hannan, Smyth *et al.*, 1996). Figure 7.5 indicates that boys are much more likely to rate themselves as "usually well ahead of classmates" than girls.

FIGURE 7.5: ACADEMIC SELF-IMAGE AMONG JUNIOR CERT PUPILS "USUALLY WELL AHEAD OF CLASSMATES"

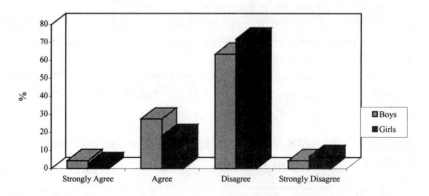

This gender difference persists even when family background and prior ability/performance are taken into account (see Tables A7.5 and A7.6). In addition, pupils from middle-class backgrounds and those whose mothers have higher levels of education tend to have a more positive view of their own abilities. At Junior Cert level, older pupils tend to have lower self-images, a pattern which may reflect being previously "kept back" in school. There may be a reciprocal relationship between lower self-confidence and under-performance at the Junior Cert (see Chapter 4) for this group. In contrast, older pupils at Leaving Cert level tend to have more positive self-ratings, perhaps reflecting greater maturity.[3]

Current evaluations of academic ability are likely to reflect positive feedback in the past. Those with higher ability levels (Junior Cert pupils) and higher grades in the Junior Cert exam (Leaving Cert pupils) tend to have a more positive view of their own abilities. In addition, those repeating the Leaving Cert have more academic self-confidence than those taking the exam for the first time (Table A7.6).

7.3.2 School social context

Interestingly, while working-class pupils tend to have more negative self-images, the social class mix of the school has the opposite effect; pupils in predominantly working-class schools

---

[3] It is also possible that this may reflect a positive impact of taking Transition Year among this group. However, it is difficult to disentangle the effects of Transition Year and age among the sample.

tend to have more self-confidence than those in middle-class schools (Table 7.3). This pattern is likely to be related to differences in the academic climate of schools (see below). The extent of differences between schools in pupil self-image are reduced when pupil composition is taken into account, although the differences remain statistically significant (see Figure 7.6).

FIGURE 7.6: ADJUSTED SCHOOL DIFFERENCES IN ACADEMIC SELF-IMAGE — JUNIOR CERT PUPILS

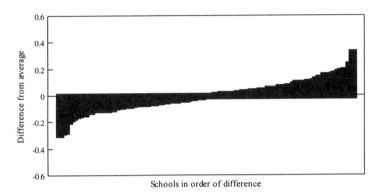

7.3.3 School type

At Junior Cert level, boys in coed schools, particularly coed secondary and vocational schools, tend to have lower academic self-images than their single-sex counterparts (Table 7.3). This pattern may reflect a greater self-consciousness among boys in coed schools about their own abilities when they compare themselves to higher-performing girls (see Hannan, Smyth *et al.*, 1996).

7.3.4 School organisation and process

There are some differences between Junior and Leaving Certificate pupils in the factors shaping their academic self-confidence. Among Junior Cert pupils, those who take fewer exam subjects tend to have a more positive view of their abilities; this pattern may reflect less academic pressure on this group (Table 7.3). At Leaving Cert level, streaming is positively associated with higher

TABLE 7.3: SCHOOL CHARACTERISTICS AND ACADEMIC SELF-IMAGE

Fixed effects	Junior Certificate			Leaving Certificate		
	Model					
	1	2	3	1	2	3
School context:						
Average social class	.113*	.128*		.123*	.104*	
School type:						
Coed Secondary		-.148*			-.049	
Coed Secondary* Girls		.192*			.147	
Vocational		-.131*			.031	
Vocational* Girls		.158*			.094	
Comm./Comp.		-.055			.058	
Comm./Comp. *Girls		.104			.028	
School organisation:						
Streaming			-			.020
Curriculum:						
Number of subjects (low)			.178*			-
Disciplinary climate:						
Homework rules			-			.079*
Strict school			-			-.047*
Pupil behaviour			-			-.193*
Interaction:						
Average positive interaction			-			.326*
Positive pupil-teacher interaction			.624*			.544*
Negative pupil-teacher interaction			-.238*			-.215*
Academic climate:						
Average teacher expectations			-.112*			-.072*
Random effects						
School-level variance	0.020*	0.018*	0.020*	0.039*	0.037*	0.014*
Pupil-level variance	0.834*	0.834*	0.689*	0.795*	0.794*	0.701*

Note: * p<.05.

All models are controlled for gender, pupil background and ability. The coefficients for pupil background and ability/performance factors are reported in Tables A7.5 and A7.6.

academic self-image as are clearly defined homework rules. Academic self-image is lower where pupils experience disruption of their learning time through pupil misconduct (Table 7.3). However, pupils also have lower self-images where they view the school as very strict; the latter pattern may be due to a stronger academic climate in strict schools (see Chapter 4).

Among both Junior and Leaving Cert pupils, positive interaction with, and feedback from, teachers is associated with enhanced self-images. At Leaving Cert level, the overall level of positive interaction between teachers and pupils has a significant impact over and above the effect on the individual pupil; that is, pupils tend to have more positive self-images in schools characterised by positive relations between teachers and pupils. Conversely, pupils tend to have less self-confidence where they themselves have experienced negative interaction with teachers. The academic climate of the school has an additional effect; pupils tend to have somewhat lower self-confidence where the overall level of teacher expectations in the school is high.

In summary, certain aspects of the schooling process, in particular the nature of teacher-pupil interaction, influence pupils' view of their own abilities. There is a reference group effect with pupils in highly academic or strict schools evaluating themselves against somewhat higher standards and consequently becoming more critical of their own academic abilities. The extent to which pupil and school differences in academic self-image directly influence academic performance will be explored in Chapter 9.

7.4 LOCUS OF CONTROL

Locus of control refers to the extent of pupils' perceived sense of control over their lives and ability to cope with problems; the scale used is described in Table A7.1. There are significant differences between schools in the extent of control which pupils feel over their lives (see Figure 7.7), although there is much greater variation at the individual pupil level. Overall, schools account for only 2 per cent of the variation in locus of control (see Table 7.1).

7.4.1 Pupil background

In general, girls tend to have lower sense of control over their lives than boys, although the effects are more apparent at Junior than at Leaving Cert level (Tables A7.7 and A7.8). Middle-class pupils tend to report a greater sense of control and ability to cope with problems than their working-class counterparts. Lower ability pupils report less sense of control over their lives than

FIGURE 7.7: "RAW" SCHOOL DIFFERENCES IN LOCUS OF CONTROL
— JUNIOR CERT PUPILS

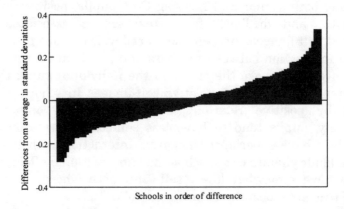

higher ability pupils. Controlling for pupil composition, schools continue to have an impact on pupils' locus of control, although the effects are small in size (see Figure 7.8).

FIGURE 7.8: ADJUSTED SCHOOL DIFFERENCES IN LOCUS OF CONTROL — JUNIOR CERT PUPILS

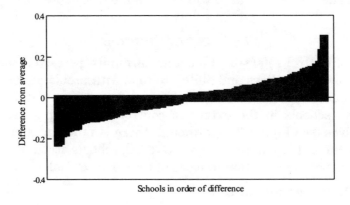

7.4.2 School characteristics

Locus of control does not vary significantly by type of school, although certain aspects of the schooling process have a significant influence. In particular, the nature of the interaction with teachers and other pupils has a crucial impact. Pupils have a greater sense of control where they report positive interaction with teachers. Conversely, pupils tend to be more fatalistic when they experience negative interaction with teachers and/or are the victims of bullying (Table 7.4). At Junior Cert level, pupils in the bottom or remedial class report a relatively low sense of control over their lives. Conversely, those taking fewer exam subjects than average report a greater sense of control.

In summary, schools have comparatively little influence on the overall variation in feelings of control among young people. However, pupils in second-level schools tend to feel more sense of control over their lives where they experience the school environment as positive.

TABLE 7.4: SCHOOL CHARACTERISTICS AND LOCUS OF CONTROL

	Junior Certificate			Leaving Certificate		
Fixed effects	Model					
	1	2	3	1	2	3
School context:						
Average social class	.058	.069*		-.012	.009	
School type:						
Coed Secondary		-.060			.009	
Coed Secondary* Girls		-.046			-.074	
Vocational		-.096			-.106	
Vocational* Girls		.019			.007	
Comm./Comp.		.088			.084	
Comm./Comp.* Girls		-.060			-.154	
School organisation:						
Bottom/ remedial class			-.124*			-
Curriculum:						
Number of subjects (low)			.093*			-
Interaction:						
Positive pupil-teacher interaction			.360*			.200*
Negative pupil-teacher interaction			-.217*			-.248*
Being bullied			-.414*			-.507*
Random effects						
School-level variance	0.017*	0.016*	0.015*	0.017*	0.015*	0.011*
Pupil-level variance	0.911*	0.911*	0.825*	0.936*	0.935*	0.878*

Note: * $p < .05$.

All models are controlled for gender, pupil background and ability. The coefficients for pupil background and ability/performance factors are reported in Tables A7.7 and A7.8.

7.5 BODY IMAGE

Pupils were asked to evaluate their personal appearance in terms of being good-looking, attractive, graceful and fat/thin. As might be expected, the extent of variation between schools, while signifi-cant, is small (5 per cent of total variation) relative to that between pupils within schools (see Figure 7.9).

FIGURE 7.9: "RAW" SCHOOL DIFFERENCES IN BODY IMAGE
— JUNIOR CERT PUPILS

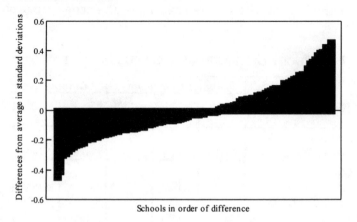

Schools in order of difference

7.5.1 Pupil background

Girls are found to have significantly lower body images than boys, a pattern which appears to be related to general cultural messages and evaluations regarding female appearance rather than to school context (see Hannan, Smyth *et al.*, 1996). In addi-tion, working-class pupils and pupils in predominantly working-class schools tend to have more negative views of their appear-ance. Higher ability/performance pupils also tend to have more negative body images (Tables A7.9 and A7.10). Taking account of pupil composition reduces the extent of variation between schools in average body image, although the difference between schools remains statistically significant (see Figure 7.10).

FIGURE 7.10: ADJUSTED SCHOOL DIFFERENCES IN BODY IMAGE
— JUNIOR CERT PUPILS

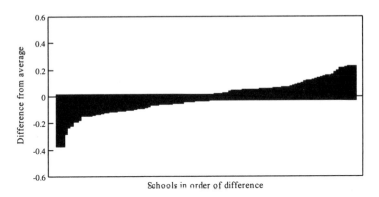

Schools in order of difference

7.5.2 School type

Being in a coeducational school tends to have a negative impact on boys' view of their own appearance. No such effect is apparent for girls (Table 7.5). Thus, being in a coed school tends to make boys more self-conscious about their abilities and their appearance while girls have more negative self-images than boys, regardless of the type of school they attend (see Hannan, Smyth *et al.*, 1996).

7.5.3 School organisation and process

Body image is also influenced by the nature of interaction within schools. Pupils who report more positive interaction with teachers and other pupils tend to have a more positive view of their own appearance. The negative impact of bullying on body image may be related to the role of "name-calling" in bullying. At Leaving Cert level, being in a bottom/remedial class is associated with more negative body image; this may relate to a greater emphasis on appearance among lower stream/ability pupils (see Hannan, Smyth *et al.*, 1996). At Junior Cert level, a positive academic climate is associated with more positive body image, although this effect is not apparent at the Leaving Cert level.

In summary, while body image varies significantly among pupils, pupils' views of their own appearance may be enhanced in a more positive school climate where they have good relations with their peers and teachers.

TABLE 7.5: SCHOOL CHARACTERISTICS AND BODY IMAGE

Fixed effects	Junior Certificate			Leaving Certificate		
	Model					
	1	2	3	1	2	3
School context:						
Average social class	-.062*	-.033		-.033	-.050	
School type:						
Coed Secondary		-.196*			-.252*	
Coed Secondary*		.203*			.322*	
Girls		-.158*			-.065	
Vocational		.095			.253	
Vocational* Girls		-.179*			-.243*	
Comm./Comp.		.238*			.315*	
Comm./Comp.* Girls			-.169*			-.210*
Coed school			.209*			.331*
Coed* Girls						
School organisation:						
Bottom/ remedial class			-			-.090*
Interaction:						
Positive pupil-teacher interaction			.269*			.299*
Being bullied			-.379*			-.352*
Academic climate:						
Average teacher expectations			.142*			-
Random effects						
School-level variance	0.018*	0.014*	0.012*	0.018*	0.010*	0.012*
Pupil-level variance	0.900*	0.900*	0.860*	0.922*	0.921*	0.884*

Note: * $p<.05$.

All models are controlled for gender, pupil background and ability. The coefficients for pupil background and ability/performance factors are reported in Tables A7.9 and A7.10.

7.6 CONCLUSIONS

This chapter has considered the impact of schools on pupil development and personal stress levels. As might be expected, there is considerably less variation between schools in average pupil development and stress than in average academic performance. However, key aspects of the schooling process have a consistent and significant effect on personal and social development among young people. In particular, the quality of relations with teachers and other pupils in the school plays a crucial role in fostering pupil development. In contrast, the existence of a formalised pastoral care programme does not have an independent effect on any of the development measures considered. It is evident, therefore, that attempts to enhance pupil development are contingent on (changes in) the broader school climate and that formal school measures to promote pupil development must take account of the broader school climate and ethos.

It is debatable whether schools can be expected to significantly enhance all aspects of personal-social development among young people. Some developmental outcomes (such as positive body image) are not an explicit goal of the schooling process. However, even in these cases, schools may represent potential sites for intervention or referral for pupils with particular problems. Other outcomes, such as academic self-image, are relative in nature, that is, pupils assess their abilities in reference to their peers. Consequently, academic self-image cannot be equally high for all pupils in the school. However, if academic self-image is found to have an impact on actual performance, low self-image among particular groups of pupils must be a matter for concern. The extent to which aspects of personal-social development may influence exam results is explored in greater detail in Chapter 9.

Appendix

TABLE A7.1: DERIVATION OF STRESS AND PERSONAL DEVELOPMENT
MEASURES

Variables	*Description*
Stress	Likert scale based on the following items: (1) Been able to concentrate on whatever you're doing (2) Felt that you were playing a moderately useful part in things (3) Felt capable of making decisions about things (4) Lost much sleep over worry (5) Felt constantly under strain (6) Been losing confidence in yourself. Reliability: alpha of 0.72 (JC) and 0.73 (LC). Original scores range from 6 to 24; the variable has been standardised to have a mean of 0 and a standard deviation of 1.
Academic Self-Image	Likert scale based on the following items: (1) I can do just about anything I set my mind to (2) I'm usually well ahead of others in my year in school (3) I am as good at school work as most other people my age (4) I'm hardly ever able to do what my teachers expect of me (reversed) (5) I'm usually well ahead of others in my class. Reliability: alpha of 0.67 (JC) and 0.68 (LC). Original scores range from 1 to 4; standardised to have a mean of 0 and a standard deviation of 1.

Locus of Control	Likert scale based on the following items: (1) I have little control over the things that happen to me (reversed) (2) There is a lot I can do to change my life if I really want to (3) I often feel helpless in trying to deal with the problems I have (reversed) (4) What happens in the future really depends on me (5) I can do just about anything I set my mind to (6) There is really no way I can solve some of the problems I have. Reliability: alpha of 0.50 (JC) and 0.53 (LC). Original scores range from 1 to 4; standardised to have a mean of 0 and a standard deviation of 1.
Body Image	Likert scale based on the pupils' selection from adjective pairs: (1) Plain – Good-looking (2) Fat – Thin (3) Awkward – Graceful (4) Unattractive – Attractive. Reliability: alpha of 0.64 (JC, LC). Original scores range from 1 to 7; standardised to have a mean of 0 and a standard deviation of 1.

TABLE A7.2: DESCRIPTIONS OF EXPLANATORY VARIABLES

Variables	Description
Pupil Background	
Gender	Dummy variable where 1= Girl.
Social class	Census Social Class scale ranging from 0 (Higher Professional) to 5 (Unskilled manual worker) based on the occupational status of parents.
Mother's education	Highest level of mother's education ranging from 0 (primary education) to 4 (university degree).
Aged 16 and over (JC)	Dummy variable where 1= Aged 16+ on 1st January 1994.
Aged 18 and over (LC)	Dummy variable where 1= Aged 18+ on 1st January 1994.
Ability / Performance	
Ability (JC)	VRNA, combined verbal reasoning and numerical ability scores; centred on its mean value.
Missing for ability test (JC)	Dummy variable where 1= Absent from school on day of VRNA test.
Junior/Inter Cert GPAV (LC)	Grade point average in Junior/Inter Cert centred on its mean value.
Inter Cert (LC)	Dummy variable where 1 = sat Inter rather than Junior Cert.
Repeating Leaving Cert (LC)	Dummy variable where 1= repeating Leaving Certificate.
School social context	
Average social class	Average social class of pupils within the school; centred on its mean value.
School organisation	
Streaming	Extent of streaming and associated curricular differentiation in the school; Guttman scale ranging from 0 (mixed ability classes) to 4 (highly streamed).
Bottom class	Dummy variable where 1= in bottom/remedial class.

Curriculum	
Number of subjects-low (JC)	Dummy variable where 1= taking <9 exam subjects.
Restricted subject choice	Dummy variable where 1= Would like to have taken a subject but could not.
Parental involvement in subject choice	School-level involvement of parents in pupils' choice of subjects; ranges from 0 (none) to 2 (high).
Disciplinary climate	
Homework rules	Extent to which the school has and enforces rules on the setting, doing and checking of homework; values range from 0 (few rules) to 2 (a number of rules which are enforced).
Pupil behaviour	Scale compiled from principal's report of frequency of discipline problems; centred on mean value.
School Interaction	
Friendly school	School-level average of pupil rating of school as "unfriendly"– "friendly"; centred on mean value.
Strict school	School-level average of pupil rating of school as "strict"–"easy-going"; centred on mean value.
Average pupil satisfaction	School-level average of pupil agreement with "For the most part, school life is a happy one for me".
Positive teacher interaction	Likert scale based on frequency of following items: (1) Have you been told that your work is good? (2) Have you been asked questions in class? (3) Have you been praised for answering a difficult question correctly? (4) Have you been praised because your written work is well done? Reliability: alpha is 0.68 (JC) and 0.67 (LC). Ranges from 0 (low) to 3 (high).
Average positive interaction	School-level average of positive teacher interaction; centred on mean.

Negative teacher interaction	Likert scale based on frequency of following items: (1) Have you been given out to because your work is untidy or not done on time? (2) Have you wanted to ask or answer questions in class but were ignored? (3) Have you been given out to for misbehaving in class? (4) Teachers pay more attention in class to what some pupils say than to others. (5) I find most teachers hard to talk to. Reliability: alpha is 0.59 (JC) and 0.61 (LC). Values range from 0 (low) to 3 (high).
Bullying	Likert scale based on frequency of following items: (1) Been jeered at or mocked by other pupils. (2) Experienced being bullied or physically pushed around by other pupils. (3) Been upset by things said about you behind your back by other pupils. (4) Been pestered or bullied on the way to or from school. Reliability: alpha is 0.64 (JC) and 0.61 (LC). Values range from 0 (low) to 2 (high).
Level of bullying	School-level average of bullying scale; centred on average.
Academic climate	
Average hours of study	School-level average of no. of hours of study/homework per night; centred on average value.
Average teacher expectations	School-level average of the highest qualification which teachers expect the pupil to get. Ranges from 1 (Junior Cert) to 4 (University Degree); centred on mean value.

TABLE A7.3: MULTI-LEVEL MODELS OF STRESS AMONG JUNIOR CERTIFICATE PUPILS (N=5,153)

Fixed effects	Model				
	1	*2*	*3*	*4*	*5*
Intercept	-.009	-.279	-.286	-.216	-.426
Pupil background:					
Gender (female)		.480*	.481*	.409*	.568*
Social class		.001	.009	.009	.005
Social class unknown		.063	.092	.084	.050
Mother's education		.011	.005	.006	.010
Parental education unknown		.007	-.002	-.001	.008
Aged 16 and over		.006	.011	.017	.002
Ability:					
VRNA score		.002*	.002*	.002*	.003*
Missing for ability test		.080	.080	.082	.036
School context:					
Average social class			-.097*	-.069*	
School type:					
Coed Secondary				-.064	
Coed Secondary* Girls				.062	
Vocational				-.133*	
Vocational* Girls				.083	
Comm./Comp.				-.110	
Comm./Comp.*Girls				.186	
Curriculum:					
Number of subjects (low)					-.113*
Restricted subject choice					.145*
Parental involvement in subject choice					.061*
Disciplinary climate:					
Homework rules					-.066*
Interaction:					
Friendly school					-.110*
Positive pupil teacher interaction[1]					-.175*
Negative pupil-teacher interaction[1]					.307*
Being bullied					.405*

Random effects:					
School-level variance	0.041*	0.015*	0.011*	0.010*	0.006*
Pupil-level variance	0.930*	0.898*	0.898*	0.897*	0.847*
Deviance	14364.7	14129.9	14118.9	14111.7	13795.0
Degrees of freedom	-	8	9	15	18
Improvement in deviance	-	<.001	<.001	n.s.	<.001

Note: * p<.05.

[1] Dummy variables for missing information on these variables were included in the analysis but are not reported here.

TABLE A7.4: MULTI-LEVEL MODELS OF STRESS AMONG LEAVING CERTIFICATE PUPILS (N=4,724)

	Model				
Fixed effects	*1*	*2*	*3*	*4*	*5*
Intercept	-.009	-.246	-.246	-.194	-.483
Pupil background:					
Gender (female)		.504*	.503*	.482*	.562*
Social class		-.003	-.002	-.002	.002
Social class unknown		-.147	-.142	-.145	-.104
Mother's education		-.022	-.023	-.023	-.027*
Parental education unknown		.145	.144	.149	.080
Aged 18 and over		.060	.060	.063	.078
Ability:					
Junior Cert GPAV[1]		.035*	.035*	.033*	.051*
Inter Cert		.121*	.111	.116	.168*
Repeating Leaving Cert		-.175*	-.169*	-.166*	-.151*
School context:					
Average social class				-.022	.001
School type:					
Coed Secondary				-.086	
Coed Secondary* Girls				.058	
Vocational				-.128	
Vocational* Girls				.026	
Comm./Comp.				-.017	
Comm./Comp.* Girls				-.027	
Curriculum:					
Restricted subject choice					.164*
Parental involvement in subject choice[1]					.050*
Disciplinary climate:					
Homework rules					-.052

Interaction:					
Average pupil satisfaction					-.186*
Positive pupil-teacher interaction[1]					-.173*
Negative pupil-teacher interaction[1]					.201*
Being bullied[1]					.571*
Academic climate:					
Average hours of study					.108*
Random effects:					
School-level variance	0.054*	0.017*	0.017*	0.015*	0.013*
Pupil-level variance	0.920*	0.883*	0.883*	0.883*	0.812*
Deviance	13145.4	12880.3	12879.9	12873.8	12473.8
Degrees of freedom	-	10	11	17	21
Improvement in deviance	-	<.001	n.s.	n.s.	<.001

Note: * p<.05.

[1] Dummy variables for missing information on these variables were included in the analysis but are not reported here.

TABLE A7.5: MULTI-LEVEL MODELS OF ACADEMIC SELF-IMAGE
AMONG JUNIOR CERT PUPILS (N=5,216)

	Model				
Fixed effects	1	2	3	4	5
Intercept	-.010	.114	.123	.211	-.403
Pupil background:					
Gender (female)		-.106*	-.111*	-.230*	-.174*
Social class		-.041*	-.050*	-.050*	-.039*
Social class unknown		-.205*	-.232*	-.233*	-.138*
Mother's education		.040*	.045*	.046*	.031*
Parental education unknown		-.008	-.002	-.0002	-.026
Aged 16 and over		-.142*	-.148*	-.143*	-.122*
Ability:					
VRNA score		.016*	.016*	.016*	.015*
Missing for ability test		-.168*	-.169*	-.167*	-.117*
School context:					
Average social class			.113*	.128*	
School type:					
Coed Secondary				-.148*	
Coed Secondary*Girls				.192*	
Vocational				-.131*	
Vocational*Girls				.158*	
Comm./Comp.				-.055	
Comm./Comp.*Girls				.104	
Curriculum:					
Number of subjects (low)					.178*
Interaction:					
Positive pupil-teacher interaction[1]					.624*
Negative pupil-teacher interaction[1]					-.238*
Academic climate:					
Average teacher expectations					-.112*
Random effects:					
School-level variance	0.031*	0.024*	0.020*	0.018*	0.020*
Pupil-level variance	0.933*	0.835*	0.834*	0.834*	0.689*
Deviance	14540.0	13950.1	13937.1	13929.6	12952.0
Degrees of freedom	-	8	9	15	14
Improvement in deviance	-	<.001	<.001	n.s.	<.001

Note: * p<.05.

[1] Dummy variables for missing information on these variables were included in the analysis but are not reported here.

TABLE A7.6: MULTI-LEVEL MODELS OF ACADEMIC SELF-IMAGE AMONG LEAVING CERT PUPILS (N=4,749)

	Model				
Fixed effects	*1*	*2*	*3*	*4*	*5*
Intercept	-0.001	0.042	0.036	0.039	-0.429
Pupil background:					
Gender (female)		-.164*	-.162*	-.232*	-.216*
Social class		-.007	-.013	-.012	-.011
Social class unknown		-.020	-.036	-.032	-.012
Mother's education		.037*	.041*	.041*	.034*
Parental education unknown		.098	.099	.091	.151
Aged 18 and over		.093*	.096*	.095*	.067
Ability:					
Junior Cert GPAV		.230*	.232*	.233*	.207*
Junior Cert results not reported		-.339*	-.334*	-.334*	-.265*
Inter Cert		.179*	.221*	.227*	.188*
Repeating Leaving Cert		.168*	.143	.134	.110
School context:					
Average social class			.123*	.104*	
School type:					
Coed Secondary				-.049	
Coed Secondary* Girls				.147	
Vocational				.031	
Vocational* Girls				.094	
Comm./Comp.				.058	
Comm./Comp.* Girls				.028	
School organisation:					
Streaming					.020
Disciplinary climate:					
Homework rules					.079*
Strict school					-.047*
Pupil behaviour					-.193*
Interaction:					
Average positive interaction					.326*
Positive pupil-teacher interaction[1]					.544*
Negative pupil-teacher interaction					-.215*
Academic climate:					
Average teacher expectations					-.072

Random effects:					
School-level variance	0.028*	0.043*	0.039*	0.037*	0.014*
Pupil-level variance	0.934*	0.795*	0.795*	0.794*	0.701*
Deviance	13242.6	12515.8	12506.9	12501.6	11854.1
Degrees of freedom	-	10	11	17	19
Improvement in deviance	-	<.001	<.01	n.s.	<.001

Note: * p<.05.

[1] Dummy variables for missing information on these variables were included in the analysis but are not reported here.

TABLE A7.7: MULTI-LEVEL MODELS OF LOCUS OF CONTROL AMONG
JUNIOR CERT PUPILS (N=5,238)

Fixed effects	Model				
	1	2	3	4	5
Intercept	-.016	.159	.164	.195	.114
Pupil background:					
Gender (female)		-.089*	-.090*	-.083	-.160*
Social class		-.028*	-.033*	-.033*	-.024*
Social class unknown		-.142	-.158*	-.162*	-.093
Mother's education		-.014	-.011	-.010	-.019
Parental education unknown		-.198*	-.194*	-.193*	-.188*
Aged 16 and over		-.199*	-.203*	-.198*	-.169*
Ability:					
VRNA score		.009*	.009*	.009*	.006†
Missing for ability test		-.112*	-.112*	-.108*	-.067
School context:					
Average social class			.058	.069*	
School type:					
Coed Secondary				-.060	
Coed Secondary* Girls				-.046	
Vocational				-.096	
Vocational* Girls				.019	
Comm./Comp.				.088	
Comm./Comp.* Girls				-.060	
School organisation:					
Bottom/remedial class					-.124*
Curriculum:					
Number of subjects (low)					.093*
Interaction:					
Positive pupil-teacher interaction[1]					.360*
Negative pupil-teacher interaction[1]					-.217*
Being bullied[1]					-.414*
Random effects:					
School-level variance	0.023*	0.018*	0.017*	0.016*	0.015*
Pupil-level variance	0.946*	0.911*	0.911*	0.911*	0.825*
Deviance	14619.4	14410.4	14406.9	14404.1	13890.1
Degrees of freedom	-	8	9	15	16
Improvement in deviance	-	<.001	<.1	n.s.	<.001

Note: * p<.05.

[1] Dummy variables for missing information on these variables were
included in the analysis but are not reported here.

TABLE A7.8: MULTI-LEVEL MODELS OF LOCUS OF CONTROL AMONG
LEAVING CERT PUPILS (N=4,752)

	Model				
Fixed effects	1	2	3	4	5
Intercept	-0.003	0.028	0.028	0.031	.228
Pupil background:					
Gender (female)		-.050	-.051	-.008	-.123*
Social class		-.007	-.006	-.005	-.009
Social class unknown		-.029	-.026	-.027	-.060
Mother's education		.004	.003	.003	.007
Parental education unknown		-.433*	-.433*	-.428*	-.403*
Aged 18 and over		.007	.006	.012	-.013
Ability:					
Junior Cert GPAV		.053*	.053*	.051*	.026*
Junior Cert results not reported		-.065	-.065	-.059	-.029
Inter Cert		.115	.109	.111	.081
Repeating Leaving Cert		.031	.034	.039	-.016
School context:					
Average social class			-.012	.009	
School type:					
Coed Secondary				.009	
Coed Secondary* Girls				-.074	
Vocational				-.106	
Vocational* Girls				.007	
Comm./Comp.				.084	
Comm./Comp.* Girls				-.154	
Interaction:					
Positive pupil-teacher interaction[1]					.200*
Negative pupil-teacher interaction					-.248*
Being bullied[1]					-.507*
Random effects:					
School-level variance	0.016*	0.017*	0.017*	0.015*	0.011*
Pupil-level variance	0.948*	0.936*	0.936*	0.935*	0.878*
Deviance	13288.3	13234.1	13234.0	13224.7	12916.2
Degrees of freedom	-	10	11	17	15
Improvement in deviance	-	<.001	n.s.	n.s.	<.001

Note: * p<.05.

[1] Dummy variables for missing information on these variables were included in the analysis but are not reported here.

TABLE A7.9: MULTI-LEVEL MODELS OF BODY IMAGE AMONG JUNIOR CERTIFICATE PUPILS (N=5,132)

	Model				
Fixed effects	*1*	*2*	*3*	*4*	*5*
Intercept	-.005	.305	.301	.417	.209
Pupil background:					
Gender (female)		-.426*	-.425*	-.549*	-.598*
Social class		-.051*	-.046*	-.046*	-.044*
Social class unknown		-.248*	-.231*	-.237*	-.210*
Mother's education		.010	.007	.007	.001
Parental education unknown		.041	.036	.039	.024
Aged 16 and over		.012	.016	.023	.045
Ability:					
VRNA score		-.004*	-.005*	-.005*	.006*
Missing for ability test		-.007	-.008	-.004	.009
School context:					
Average social class			-.062*	-.033	
School type:					
Coed Secondary				-.196*	
Coed Secondary* Girls				.203*	
Vocational				-.158*	
Vocational* Girls				.095	
Comm./Comp.				-.179*	
Comm./Comp.* Girls				.238*	
Coed School					-.169*
Coed School* Girls					.209*
Interaction:					
Positive pupil-teacher interaction[1]					.269*
Being bullied[1]					-.379*
Academic climate:					
Average teacher expectations					.142*
Random effects:					
School-level variance	0.049*	0.019*	0.018*	0.014*	0.012*
Pupil-level variance	0.927*	0.901*	0.900*	0.900*	0.860*
Deviance	14304.7	14098.0	14094.0	14081.1	13843.2
Degrees of freedom	-	8	9	15	15
Improvement in deviance	-	<.001	<.05	<.05	<.001

Note: * p<.05.

[1] Dummy variables for missing information on these variables were included in the analysis but are not reported here.

TABLE A7.10: MULTI-LEVEL MODELS OF BODY IMAGE AMONG
LEAVING CERTIFICATE PUPILS (N=4,714)

	Model				
Fixed effects	1	2	3	4	5
Intercept	.007	.111	.112	.238	.031
Pupil background:					
Gender (female)		-.309*	-.310*	-.517*	-.582*
Social class		-.009	-.007	-.008	-.008
Social class unknown		.015	.022	.027	.011
Mother's education		.045*	.044*	.045*	.044*
Parental education unknown		-.090	-.091	-.105	-.045
Aged 18 and over		.106*	.105*	.109*	.113*
Ability:					
Junior Cert GPAV		-.025*	-.026*	-.025*	-.040*
Junior Cert GPAV not reported		-.140	-.141	-.137	-.097
Inter Cert		-.012	-.027	-.029	-.019
Repeating Leaving Cert		.002	.011	-.002	-.045
School context:					
Average social class			-.033	-.050	
School type:					
Coed Secondary				-.252*	
Coed Secondary* Girls				.322*	
Vocational				-.065	
Vocational* Girls				.253	
Comm./Comp.				-.243*	
Comm./Comp.* Girls				.315*	
Coed School					-.210*
Coed School* Girls					.331*
School organisation:					
Bottom/remedial class					-.090*
Interaction:					
Positive pupil-teacher interaction[1]					.299*
Being bullied[1]					-.352*
Random effects:					
School-level variance	0.047*	0.018*	0.018*	0.010*	0.012*
Pupil-level variance	0.933*	0.922*	0.922*	0.921*	0.884*
Deviance	13173.3	13060.6	13059.7	13032.9	12844.1
Degrees of freedom	-	10	11	17	17
Improvement in deviance	-	<.001	n.s.	<.001	<.001

Note: * p<.05.

[1] Dummy variables for missing information on these variables were
included in the analysis but are not reported here.

Chapter 8

DIFFERENTIAL EFFECTIVENESS

The analyses in Chapters 4 and 5 were concerned with the influence of school-level factors on academic performance for the "average" pupil. However, previous research in the British and American contexts has indicated that the "effectiveness" of a school may differ according to the type of pupil considered. These studies indicate that schools may not be equally effective for pupils of different ability levels, for girls and boys, and/or for pupils of different ethnic backgrounds (Sammons *et al.*, 1997; Nuttall *et al.*, 1989; Smith and Tomlinson, 1989; Bryk and Raudenbush, 1988). This chapter examines whether second-level schools in Ireland are equally effective in promoting academic progress among different groups of pupils at Junior and Leaving Certificate level.

This analysis is carried out in two ways. First, the impact of pupil characteristics is allowed to vary across schools in order to test whether the relationship between gender, for example, and exam performance is the same in all schools.[1] Second, tests are carried out to assess whether key factors of school organisation and process have different effects on different groups of pupils; for example, whether teacher expectations have stronger effects on boys than on girls.

---

[1] This kind of model is termed a "fully random model" where both the intercept and the slope are allowed to be random; the models presented in Chapters 4 to 7 are "random intercepts models" (see Chapter 2).

8.1 JUNIOR CERTIFICATE EXAM PERFORMANCE

8.1.1 Prior ability

Table 8.1 presents a series of multi-level models which test whether schools are equally effective for pupils of different prior ability levels. Model 1 indicates that schools vary significantly from each other in terms of pupil exam performance but assumes that schools are equally effective for higher and lower ability pupils (see Chapter 4).

TABLE 8.1: DIFFERENTIAL EFFECTIVENESS BY PRIOR ABILITY AT JUNIOR CERTIFICATE LEVEL

Random effects	Model 1	Model 2	Model 3
School-level variance			
Intercept	0.161*	0.166*	0.168*
Covariance	-	-.002*	-.002*
VRNA variance	-	.0001*	.0001*
Pupil-level variance			
Intercept	1.284*	1.265*	1.303*
Covariance	-	-	-.014*
Deviance	16229.9	16204.8	15895.4
Improvement in deviance	-	<.001	<.001

Note: * indicates significance at the <.05 level.

All models control for gender, pupil background and ability factors.

Model 2 relaxes this assumption, allowing the relationship between prior ability and Junior Cert exam performance to vary across schools. This model indicates that not only do schools vary significantly in the average exam performance of their pupils but that they also vary significantly in terms of the achievement difference between higher and lower ability pupils. The covariance term indicates that the gap between higher and lower ability pupils tends to be reduced in more academically effective schools. The total variation in Junior Cert exam performance at the school level is mapped in Figure 8.1. It is evident that variation between schools is much greater for lower ability pupils than for those of average or above average ability, that is, schools make more of a difference for lower ability pupils.

FIGURE 8.1: BETWEEN-SCHOOL VARIANCE AS A FUNCTION OF PRIOR ABILITY — JUNIOR CERT

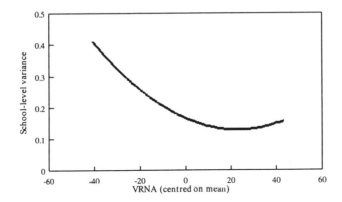

Model 3 allows for pupil-level variation by prior ability. The co-variance term indicates that higher ability pupils are less variable in their exam performance than lower ability pupils, all else being equal. School-level variation does not change appreciably when within-school variation is allowed for. Figure 8.2 shows that between-school variation as a proportion of total variance is higher at the extremes of the ability range.

FIGURE 8.2: SCHOOL AND PUPIL-LEVEL VARIANCE BY PRIOR ABILITY — JUNIOR CERT

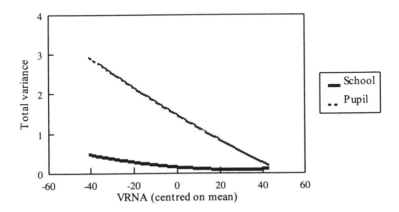

This pattern is also evident from Figure 8.3 which illustrates the slope for each of the schools in the sample, although it is evident that the variance from the average relationship between prior

ability and performance is more marked among the lower ability range.[2]

FIGURE 8.3: PREDICTED SLOPES FOR THE SAMPLED SCHOOLS
— JUNIOR CERT

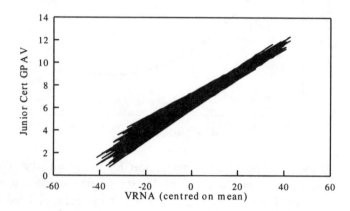

Testing for interaction effects between school characteristics and pupil ability indicates that a number of factors have a somewhat weaker effect on the exam performance of higher ability pupils than on that of their lower ability counterparts. In particular, allocation to top and middle classes[3], average negative interaction between teachers and pupils, and teachers' expectations, tend to have a stronger impact on lower than higher ability pupils. Thus, the greater difference between schools for lower ability pupils depicted in Figure 8.3 reflects the fact that certain school characteristics narrow the performance gap between higher and lower ability pupils. Taking account of this pattern explains much of the

---

[2] This pattern is confirmed by separate analyses of low, middle and high ability pupils which indicate a much lower intra-school correlation for high ability pupils. In other words, a smaller proportion of the total variance in exam performance among high ability pupils is attributable to the school level.

[3] It should be noted that this refers to the effect of a particular factor. The actual distribution of lower ability pupils across school characteristics may differ significantly from that of higher ability pupils.

differential effectiveness by ability level apparent at the school and pupil levels.

8.1.2 Gender

Table 8.2 presents a series of models which test whether schools are differentially effective for boys and girls. The individual terms for school-level variation by gender are found to be statistically insignificant; that is, the "gender gap" in performance is similar across schools (Model 2, Table 8.2). Pupil-level variation indicates that, while girls' exam performance is on average higher than that of boys, it is significantly less variable (Model 3). Thus, boys are more likely than girls to score extremely high, or extremely low, exam grades.

A better fit is achieved by allowing for school-level variation in terms of ability and pupil-level variation in terms of both ability and gender (Model 4). Thus, schools are found to vary significantly in the performance gap by prior ability level. Furthermore, higher ability pupils have less variable exam scores than those of lower ability. Girls' exam scores are less variable than those of boys, irrespective of their prior ability level.

TABLE 8.2: DIFFERENTIAL EFFECTIVENESS BY GENDER AT JUNIOR CERTIFICATE LEVEL

Random effects	*Model 1*	*Model 2*	*Model 3*	*Model 4*
School-level variance				
Intercept	0.161*	0.174*	0.170*	0.167*
Covariance				
(intercept/gender)	-	-0.025	-0.020	-
Gender variance	-	0.030	0.031	-
Covariance (intercept/VRNA)				-0.002*
VRNA variance				0.001*
Pupil-level variance				
Intercept	1.284*	1.280*	1.386*	1.451*
Covariance				
(intercept/gender)	-	-	-0.103*	-0.144*
Covariance (intercept/VRNA)				-0.015*
Deviance	16229.9	16227.4	16211.4	15852.9
Improvement in deviance[1]	-	n.s.	<.001	<.001

Note: * indicates significance at the <.05 level.

All models control for gender, pupil background and prior ability.

[1] This refers to improvement over the null model.

Additional analyses were conducted to test for interactions between school characteristics and gender. No such interaction effects were found; therefore, factors that serve to enhance Junior Certificate performance do so equally for boys and girls.

8.1.3 Social class background

Additional analyses were carried out to test whether the relationship between social class background and pupil performance varies across schools, that is, whether some schools tend to minimise (or maximise) the difference between middle-class and working-class pupils. No significant variation in the effect of social class by school was found. In addition, no significant interaction between school characteristics and pupil social class was found. Thus, being allocated to the bottom/remedial class within a streamed school has a negative effect on performance for both middle-class and working-class pupils. [4]

8.2 LEAVING CERTIFICATE EXAM PERFORMANCE

8.2.1 Prior performance

Table 8.3 presents a series of multi-level models which test whether schools are equally effective for different categories of prior achievement among Leaving Certificate pupils. Pupils who had previously taken the Intermediate, rather than the Junior, Certificate are excluded from the following analyses. Model 2 indicates that schools do in fact vary in academic effectiveness according to prior achievement of the pupils. Thus, the relationship between Junior and Leaving Cert performance in some schools is "flatter" in some schools than in others. As at Junior Certificate level, between-school differences are greater for pupils with initially lower levels of ability/performance (Figure 8.4).

---

[4] This is not to say, however, that the distribution of pupils across streamed classes does not differ for middle-class and working-class pupils.

TABLE 8.3: DIFFERENTIAL EFFECTIVENESS AT LEAVING CERTIFICATE
BY PRIOR ACHIEVEMENT AT JUNIOR CERTIFICATE

Random effects	Model 1	Model 2	Model 3
School-level variance			
Intercept	0.588*	0.650*	0.634*
Covariance	-	0.041	0.014
Prior performance variance	-	0.190*	0.192*
Pupil-level variance			
Intercept	5.311*	4.897*	4.952*
Covariance	-	-	-0.195*
Deviance	19398.9	19219.6	19201.8
Improvement in deviance	-	<.001	<.001

Note: * indicates significance at the <.05 level.

All models are controlled for gender, pupil background and prior performance at Junior Cert.

FIGURE 8.4: BETWEEN-SCHOOL VARIANCE IN PERFORMANCE
LEAVING CERT

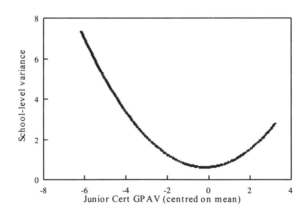

However, unlike at Junior Cert level, there is no relationship
between overall academic effectiveness and a tendency to minimise the difference between higher and lower ability pupils. Thus,
knowing that a school is "effective" for lower ability pupils tells us
little about the level of academic progress over the senior cycle
among higher ability pupils. Model 3 indicates that, as among
Junior Cert pupils, higher ability pupils tend to be less variable in
their exam performance than lower ability pupils (see also Figure
8.5).

FIGURE 8.5: SCHOOL- AND PUPIL-LEVEL VARIANCE AT LEAVING
CERT

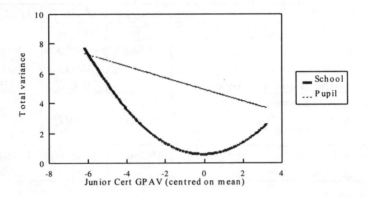

Figure 8.6 shows the different relationships (slopes) between prior
achievement and Leaving Certificate performance for each of the
schools in the sample. As at Junior Cert level, there is some
evidence of "fanning" at the lower ability range, that is, greater
difference between schools for lower-performing pupils.

FIGURE 8.6: PREDICTED SLOPES FOR THE SAMPLED SCHOOLS
— LEAVING CERT

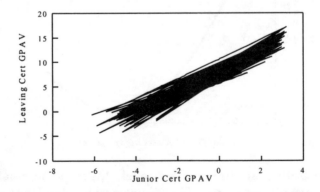

Additional analyses indicated that school factors interact with
initial ability levels in influencing Leaving Certificate performance. In particular, the impact of class allocation, formal pupil involvement, along with teacher expectations, differs for lower and
higher ability pupils. Allowing for these interaction effects helps
to explain the differential effectiveness by ability level found in
Leaving Cert performance.

8.2.2 Gender

In contrast to the findings at Junior Cert level, there appears to be significant variation between schools in the gender gap between boys and girls at Leaving Cert level (Model 2, Table 8.4). Within schools, exam performance is less variable among girls than among boys.

TABLE 8.4: DIFFERENTIAL EFFECTIVENESS BY GENDER AT LEAVING CERTIFICATE LEVEL

Random effects	Model 1	Model 2	Model 3	Model 4
School-level variance				
Intercept	0.588*	0.746*	0.719*	0.732*
Covariance (intercept/gender)	-	-0.320*	-0.291*	-0.231
Gender variance	-	0.512*	0.514*	0.408*
Covariance (intercept/ability)	-	-	-	0.023
JC score variance	-	-	-	0.207*
Covariance (gender/ability)				-0.025
Pupil-level variance				
Intercept	5.311*	5.238*	5.820*	5.523*
Covariance (intercept/gender)	-	-	-0.551*	-0.532*
Covariance (intercept/ability)	-	-	-	-0.025
Covariance (gender/ability)	-	-	-	-0.308*
Deviance	19398.9	19381.3	19359.2	19136.5
Improvement in deviance	-	<.001	<.001	<.001

Note: * indicates significance at the <.05 level.

All models are controlled for gender, pupil background and Junior Cert performance.

Allowing between-school differences to vary by gender and ability significantly improves the fit of the model. Model 4 indicates that the difference in Leaving Cert performance between girls and boys and between pupils of different ability levels varies by school. However, there is no significant relationship between these two dimensions; that is, schools that minimise the differences between higher and lower ability pupils do not necessarily minimise the difference between girls and boys. The coefficients for pupil-level variance indicate that girls are significantly less variable than boys. In addition, while higher ability pupils tend to be less variable than lower ability pupils, this decline in variability with increasing ability is much stronger for girls than for boys.

No interaction effects are apparent between school characteristics and pupil gender. Thus, for example, a higher average level of negative interaction between teachers and pupils is associated with lower exam performance for both girls and boys.

8.2.3 Social class background

As at Junior Certificate level, no significant differences are found between schools in the relationship between social class background and exam performance. In general, there are no significant interactions between school characteristics and social class. The exception to this is a weaker effect from average (and individual) teachers' expectations for working-class pupils; that is, a strong academic climate in the school appears to be of more benefit to middle-class pupils than to their working-class counterparts. This pattern is not evident for Junior Certificate pupils, however.

8.3 CONCLUSIONS

There is some evidence that second-level schools in Ireland are differentially effective for different sub-groups of pupils. This pattern is particularly evident for pupils of different prior ability/performance levels where schools are found to be significantly more variable in their effects on lower ability pupils at both Junior and Leaving Cert levels. In other words, schools make more of a difference to exam performance among lower ability pupils. There is also some evidence that, at senior cycle, some schools minimise the difference in academic performance between boys and girls while others maximise this difference. However, schools that reduce the difference between ability groups do not necessarily reduce the difference between girls and boys. It is clear, therefore, that "effectiveness" is not a uni-dimensional concept but must be regarded as group-specific. The extent to which "effectiveness" must be regarded as outcome-specific will be discussed in Chapters 9 and 10.

Chapter 9

SCHOOLING AND PUPIL OUTCOMES — A MULTIDIMENSIONAL ANALYSIS

A range of pupil outcomes, both academic and non-academic, have been considered separately in Chapters 4 to 7. It is evident that schools make more of a difference to academic outcomes, such as performance and drop-out, than to personal/social development among pupils. However, it would also be interesting to determine whether school effectiveness can be regarded as uni-dimensional, that is, whether schools that are effective in academic terms are equally effective in terms of pupil development. This chapter explores the extent to which these outcomes are inter-related at the school and pupil level.

9.1 PUPIL OUTCOMES AT JUNIOR CERTIFICATE LEVEL

Tables 9.1 and 9.2 present multivariate multilevel models where the seven pupil outcomes considered separately in Chapters 4 to 7 are modelled simultaneously as functions of the explanatory variables.[1] A multivariate approach maximises the use of available data since there is no requirement that information be available for each pupil on all seven of the outcomes. The advantage of using a multivariate approach is that it allows us to examine the interrelationships among the outcomes at both the school and pupil level. Consequently, the discussion in this chapter focuses on the random effects; coefficients for the fixed effects, including, for example, the impact of gender and social class, are the same as those presented in Chapters 4 to 7.

Table 9.1 presents the null model which indicates the school- and pupil-level variation before allowing for differences between

---

[1] This is carried out in terms of a three level model with schools treated as level 3 units, pupils as level 2 units and the "within student" measurements (the seven pupil outcomes) as level 1 units. The model is a mixed response model since some of the outcomes are continuous and some are discrete (i.e., absenteeism and potential drop-out).

schools in pupil intake. The school-level variances (shown on the diagonal) indicate that schools differ significantly from each other in exam performance, absenteeism, potential drop-out, stress, academic self-image, sense (locus) of control and body image at Junior Certificate level. This is consistent with the patterns found using the separate models presented in Chapters 4, 6 and 7.

In general, academic outcomes are significantly interrelated at school level; schools in which average exam performance is higher have significantly lower levels of absenteeism ($r = -0.52$) and drop-out ($r = -0.89$). There are also significant relationships among some measures of personal/social development; schools in which academic self-image is higher also tend to have higher average locus of control ($r = 0.75$) and body image ($r = 0.75$). However, the associations among enhanced pupil outcomes are not always consistent; for example, average stress levels are significantly higher in higher-performing schools ($r = 0.28$).

Academic outcomes are also interrelated at the pupil level. Pupils who do well in the Junior Cert are more likely to have good attendance records and less likely to intend to leave school early ($r = -0.43$). Measures of personal/social development are correlated with each other; pupils with higher academic self-image have more positive feelings of control ($r = 0.45$) and body image ($r = 0.15$). Both academic self-image and locus of control are positively associated with pupil performance, although higher-performing pupils tend to have higher stress levels and more negative body images.

Table 9.1 shows the "raw" relationships between the different pupil outcomes. However, the relationships among outcomes may be spurious; for example, the positive relationship between exam performance and stress at the school level may reflect a greater concentration of girls (who have higher exam scores and stress levels) in certain schools rather than reflecting a school effect *per se*. The model presented in Table 9.2 includes pupil background and ability in order to allow for differences between schools in pupil intake. In general, there are fewer significant interrelationships among pupil outcomes, especially at school level, in this adjusted model.

At school level, academic outcomes are significantly interrelated with higher performing schools having lower absenteeism ($r = -0.35$) and drop-out rates ($r = -0.52$), even when pupil

TABLE 9.1: MULTIVARIATE MODEL OF PUPIL OUTCOMES AT JUNIOR CERTIFICATE: NULL MODEL

	GPAV	Absenteeism	Potential drop-out	Stress	Academic self-image	Locus of control	Body image
				Pupil Outcomes			
Random effects							
School-level							
GPAV	0.816*						
Absenteeism	-0.52*	0.649*					
Potential drop-out	-0.89*	0.50*	0.499*				
Stress	0.38*	-0.12	-0.58*	0.013*			
Academic self-image	0.25	-0.16	-0.17	-0.22	0.006*		
Locus of control	0.34*	-0.05	-0.41*	-0.07	0.75*	0.004*	
Body image	0.09	-0.21	0.16	-0.59*	0.75*	0.30	0.058*
Pupil-level							
GPAV	2.869*						
Absenteeism	-0.30*	1.0					
Potential drop-out	-0.43*	0.23*	1.0				
Stress	0.04*	0.03	0.02	0.258*			
Academic self-image	0.40*	-0.15*	-0.25*	-0.13*	0.178*		
Locus of control	0.20*	-0.08*	-0.17*	-0.33*	0.45*	0.157*	
Body image	-0.08*	0.02	0.04*	-0.22*	0.15*	0.16*	1.046*
Deviance				47762.7			

Note: Variances on diagonal (bold), correlations off-diagonal.

TABLE 9.2: MULTIVARIATE MODEL OF PUPIL OUTCOMES AT JUNIOR CERTIFICATE: ADJUSTED MODEL.

	Pupil outcomes						
	GPAV	*Absenteeism*	*Drop-out*	*Stress*	*Academic S.I.*	*Control*	*Body image*
Random effects							
School-level							
GPAV	**0.157***						
Absenteeism	-0.35*	**0.628***					
Potential drop-out	-0.52*	0.41*	**0.156***				
Stress	-0.08	-0.12	-0.40	**0.006***			
Academic self-image	-0.08	0.07	0.11	-0.04	**0.006***		
Locus of control	0.00	0.18	-0.34	-0.12	0.65*	**0.004***	
Body image	0.39	-0.20	0.01	0.02	0.30	0.12	**0.003***
Pupil-level							
GPAV	**0.993***						
Absenteeism	-0.21*	**1.0**					
Potential drop-out	-0.25*	0.14*	**1.0**				
Stress	0.01	0.04*	0.06*	**0.249***			
Academic self-image	0.23*	-0.08*	-0.17*	-0.15*	**0.155***		
Locus of control	0.10*	-0.04*	-0.13*	-0.34*	0.42*	**0.152***	
Body image	0.00	0.00	0.02	-0.20*	0.18*	0.17*	**1.013***
Deviance				41360.1			

Note: Variances on diagonal (bold), correlations off-diagonal.

All models are controlled for gender, social background and prior abilty.

background and ability are taken into account (Table 9.2). The reduced size of the effects compared to the "raw" correlations, however, indicates that many schools deviate from this pattern. Some schools may, for example, enhance pupil performance while at the same time failing to reduce pupil drop-out. Measures of personal/social development are not strongly interrelated at school level. However, schools that promote academic self-image also tend to promote locus of control among pupils. There are no longer any significant interrelationships between academic and non-academic outcomes so schools that promote pupil performance do not necessarily have positive effects on pupil development. In addition, the positive relationship between average performance and stress levels evident from the "raw" results is no longer evident. There is, therefore, no necessary "trade-off" between academic effectiveness and raised stress levels among pupils.

At the pupil level, the relationships among outcome measures are broadly similar, even when adjustments are made for pupil background and ability. Pupils who do well in the Junior Cert tend to have other positive academic and non-academic outcomes (with the exception of body image). This relationship will be discussed in greater detail below.

9.2 PUPIL OUTCOMES AT LEAVING CERTIFICATE LEVEL

Tables 9.3 and 9.4 present multivariate models for pupil outcomes at Leaving Cert level. In contrast to Junior Cert, only one academic outcome, exam performance, is measured at Leaving Cert level. In terms of "raw" outcomes, the school-level variances indicate that schools differ significantly in terms of academic performance, stress levels, academic self-image, locus of control and body image (Table 9.3).

There are some significant interrelationships among pupil outcomes. At school level, higher-performing schools have higher average stress levels ($r = 0.4$). Effects on personal/social development tend to be consistent across schools. For example, schools with lower stress levels tend to have more positive academic self-images ($r = -0.4$) and body images ($r = -0.82$) on average. At pupil level, higher performing pupils tend to have more positive views of their abilities ($r = 0.41$) and control over their lives ($r = 0.11$) but more negative body images ($r = -0.05$) and higher stress levels ($r = 0.04$).

TABLE 9.3: MULTIVARIATE MODEL OF PUPIL OUTCOMES AT LEAVING CERTIFICATE: NULL MODEL

| | *Pupil outcomes* | | | | |
	GPAV	*Stress*	*Academic Self-image*	*Locus of control*	*Body image*
Random effects					
School-level					
GPAV	**3.747***				
Stress	0.40*	**0.015***			
Academic self-image	0.24	-0.40*	**0.005***		
Locus of control	0.20	0.13	0.65*	**0.002***	
Body image	-0.18	-0.82*	0.49*	0.19	**0.042***
Pupil-level					
GPAV	**15.140***				
Stress	0.04*	**0.263***			
Academic self-image	0.41*	-0.15*	**0.180***		
Locus of control	0.11*	-0.29*	0.10*	**0.112***	
Body image	-0.05*	-0.17*	0.18*	0.12*	**0.836***
Deviance	53228.7				

Note: Variances on diagonal (bold), correlations off-diagonal.

Table 9.4 presents the same model adjusted for differences between schools in pupil intake (gender, social background and prior achievement). The school-level variances indicate that schools vary significantly in academic and personal/social development, even when differences in pupil composition are taken into account. This pattern is consistent with that indicated by the separate models in Chapters 5 and 7. At school level, average performance is not significantly related to other pupil outcomes, that is, academically effective schools do not necessarily promote pupil development. However, the relationships among aspects of pupil development are more consistent, that is, schools that tend to promote self-image among pupils also tend to promote sense of control (r = 0.74) and body image (r = 0.43) and to reduce stress levels (r = -0.44). At the pupil level, higher performing pupils tend to have more positive outcomes on measures of personal/social development. The relationship between personal/social development and pupil performance is discussed in greater detail in the following section.

TABLE 9.4: MULTIVARIATE MODEL OF PUPIL OUTCOMES AT LEAVING
CERTIFICATE: ADJUSTED MODEL

| | *Pupil Outcomes* | | | | |
	GPAV	*Stress*	*Academic self-image*	*Locus of control*	*Body image*
Random effects					
School-level					
GPAV	**0.718***				
Stress	0.09	**0.005***			
Academic self-image	0.10	-0.44*	**0.008***		
Locus of control	0.31	0.01	0.74*	**0.002***	
Body image	0.14	-0.46*	0.43*	0.37	**0.016***
Pupil-level					
GPAV	**5.444***				
Stress	-0.01	**0.253***			
Academic self-image	0.20*	-0.17*	**0.154***		
Locus of control	0.05*	-0.30*	0.06*	**0.117***	
Body image	-0.05*	-0.15*	0.20*	0.12*	**0.826***
Deviance	48006.5				

Note: Variances on diagonal (bold), correlations off-diagonal.
All models are controlled for gender, social background and prior
performance.

9.3 PUPIL OUTCOMES AND ACADEMIC PERFORMANCE

9.3.1 Junior certificate exam performance

The previous section considered whether school effects operate in
a similar manner for academic and non-academic outcomes among
pupils at Junior and Leaving Certificate level. This section
examines the association between pupil outcomes (such as absenteeism, potential drop-out and personal/social development) and
academic performance. Pupil absenteeism, intended drop-out,
stress, academic self-image, locus of control and body image were
measured four months prior to the pupils sitting their examination so they can be regarded as having a potential influence on

exam outcomes.[2] While academic and non-academic outcomes may not be strongly related at the school level (see above), schools may influence performance at pupil level by shaping developmental outcomes.

Table 9.5 presents data on academic performance at Junior Certificate level. Those pupils who have poor attendance records are significantly less likely to do well in their Junior Cert exams, scoring over half a grade per subject lower than their counterparts, all else being equal. In addition, pupils who intend to leave school after the Junior Cert do worse in their exams than those who intend to remain in school, even when prior ability and other aspects of pupil background are controlled. This is likely to reflect a lower investment in studying for exams among those who intend to leave. However, the causal relationship is likely to be complex; pupils who intend to leave school early may also be responding to previous underachievement in school exams and consequent alienation from the schooling system.

Academic self-image is positively associated with exam performance at Junior Cert level, that is, pupils who have a more positive view of their own abilities tend to do better in exams. Again the relationship is likely to be complex since pupils who have previously done well in exams will have a more positive view of their abilities which in turn will affect their future performance.

Body-image is negatively associated with exam performance, although the effect is very small.[3] Locus of control has no significant effect on exam performance, when other pupil outcomes are taken into account. Contrary to what might be expected, pupil stress levels are positively associated with exam performance. Stress is associated with other factors, such as parental pressure and hours of homework/study, which are likely to be positively correlated with academic performance (see Hannan, Smyth *et al.*,

---

[2] In reality, the causal relationships are likely to be more complex with earlier academic performance over the junior cycle influencing these outcomes which in turn influence Junior Cert results.

[3] This may be related to the impact of other factors which influence body image. For example, pupils with a more active social life tend to have more positive body images (see Hannan, Smyth *et al.*, 1996); this may have a detrimental effect on pupil performance. Therefore, the coefficient may reflect the influence of other factors rather than the negative impact of body image *per se*.

1996). The pattern may, therefore, reflect these underlying factors rather than a "positive" effect of stress.[4] These patterns hold when aspects of school organisation and process are taken into account (Model 2, Table 9.5).

Some aspects of pupil background are reduced in significance when pupil outcomes are considered. Factors, such as social class, mother's education, gender, age and ability, appear to be partially mediated by absenteeism, potential drop-out and personal/social development. Thus, middle-class pupils tend to do better in exams in part because they have better attendance, are more likely to intend to stay on in school, and have more positive self-images. However, pupil background continues to directly affect performance even when these other outcomes are taken into account.

TABLE 9.5: PUPIL OUTCOMES AND JUNIOR CERT EXAM
PERFORMANCE

Fixed effects	*Model 1*	*Model 2*
Pupil outcomes[1]		
Absenteeism	-.529*	-.507*
Potential drop-out	-.661*	-.576*
Academic self-image	.566*	.646*
Body-image	-.044*	-.046*
Locus of control	.048	.018
Stress	.128*	.116*
Random effects		
School-level variance		
Intercept	0.151*	0.091*
Pupil-level variance		
Intercept	1.088*	0.937*
Deviance	15364.0	14791.7
Degrees of freedom	21	35
Improvement in deviance over null model	<.001	<.001

Note: * significant at the <.05 level.
Model 1 controls for pupil background; Model 2 for background and school organisation/process.
[1.] Dummy variables for missing information were included but are not reported here.

---

[4] There also appears to be evidence of a threshold effect; those with extremely high stress levels do not do significantly better in the Junior Cert than those with lower levels.

9.3.2 Leaving Certificate exam performance

Data on the association between pupil outcomes and Leaving Cert performance are presented in Table 9.6. As at Junior Cert level, academic self-image is strongly associated with exam performance while body-image is negatively associated with Leaving Cert results. In contrast to the pattern at Junior Cert, pupils with stronger feelings of control over their lives (locus of control) tend to do better in their exams. Stress is positively associated with exam results but this pattern appears to be related to the high correlation between stress and level of educational aspiration.[5]

TABLE 9.6: PUPIL OUTCOMES AND LEAVING CERT PERFORMANCE

Fixed effects	Model 1	Model 2
Pupil outcomes[1]		
Academic self-image	1.314*	1.331*
Body-image	-.243*	-.247*
Locus of control	.404*	.386*
Stress	.143*	.142*
Random effects		
School-level variance		
Intercept	0.703*	0.456*
Pupil-level variance		
Intercept	5.135*	5.093*
Deviance	21088.9	21012.9
Degrees of freedom	18	32
Improvement in deviance over null model	<.001	<.001

Note: * significant at the <.05 level.

Model 1 controls for pupil background; Model 2 for background and school organisation/process.

[1.] Dummy variables are included for missing information but are not reported here.

---

[5] In a separate analysis, stress was found to be non-significant when pupil's level of educational aspiration was entered into the model. Thus, stress is associated with exam performance because pupils with higher aspirations tend to be more highly stressed.

9.4 CONCLUSIONS

Analyses in this chapter indicate that "effectiveness" must be seen as outcome-specific since schools that promote academic progress among pupils do not necessarily enhance their personal/social development. There is some indication that a dimension of academic effectiveness can be identified, that is, higher-performing schools tend to have lower absenteeism and drop-out rates. Similarly, there is some consistency among non-academic outcomes with significant interrelationships evident among academic self-image, body image and locus of control. Analyses at the pupil level indicate that pupils tend to do better in their exams when they have a better attendance record, intend to stay on at school and have a more positive image of themselves. Consequently, attention within schools to the promotion of "non-academic" outcomes may in fact have positive effects on academic performance among individual pupils.

This chapter indicates that there is no necessary relationship between academic effectiveness and developmental effectiveness at the school level. However, it is possible that a small number of schools may be effective (or ineffective) across a range of pupil outcomes. The extent to which consistently "effective" or "ineffective" schools can be identified is discussed in the following chapter.

Chapter 10

OUTLIER SCHOOLS

The previous chapters have examined the relationship between aspects of school organisation and pupil outcomes averaged over all schools. This chapter explores the extent to which certain schools differ significantly from the average. Chapter 11 will present detailed findings from case-studies of a number of these outlier schools.

10.1 JUNIOR CERTIFICATE

For each of the pupil outcomes discussed in Chapters 4 to 7, it is possible to calculate a school-level residual, that is, a measure which assesses the extent to which a particular school differs from the average. An outlier school is a school which is significantly above (or below) the average for all schools. Table 10.1 indicates the number of outlier schools for each of the pupil outcomes at Junior Cert level.

As indicated in Chapters 4 to 7, there is greater variation among schools in relation to academic outcomes, especially exam performance, than in relation to measures of personal/social development. The first column in Table 10.1 presents outliers based on "raw" results, indicating that pupil performance is significantly above average in 28 schools and significantly below average in 27 schools. These are the schools that would be distinguished as "effective" (or "ineffective") if a "league table" approach was used.

The next three columns control progressively for pupil background (gender, parental social class, mother's education, and age), ability (performance in VRNA test) and social context (average social class) of the school. Introducing these controls reduces the number of schools that are identified as outliers, that is, there are fewer differences between schools when adjustments are made for pupil intake. Column 4 (Table 10.1) indicates that, controlling for differences in pupil intake, 21 schools are "academically effective" while 15 schools are "academically ineffective".

Different schools are identified as effective or ineffective according to the pupil intake factors that are taken into account.

TABLE 10.1: NUMBER OF OUTLIER SCHOOLS BY OUTCOMES AMONG JUNIOR CERT PUPILS

	"Raw" scores		Adjusted for pupil background		Adjusted for pupil background + ability		Adjusted for background, ability + social context	
	E	I	E	I	E	I	E	I
Junior Cert GPAV	28	27	26	21	25	22	21	15
Absenteeism	21	23	13	23	13	22	9	17
Potential drop-out	12	20	7	10	1	2	1	2
Stress	7	10	0	3	0	1	0	1
Academic self-image	9	4	3	1	4	4	3	4
Locus of control	5	2	3	2	2	1	2	2
Body image	13	8	3	2	4	2	4	2
Total number of schools	106		106		106		106	

Note: E= "effective", i.e., significantly associated with enhanced pupil outcomes;

I= "ineffective", i.e., significantly associated with reduced pupil outcomes.

TABLE 10.2: "ADJUSTED" BY "RAW" OUTLIERS FOR JUNIOR CERT PERFORMANCE

Adjusted results	Outliers on "raw" results		
	Effective	Average	Ineffective
Effective	13	6	1
Average	14	37	20
Ineffective	1	8	6
Total	28	51	27

Of the 28 schools considered effective in terms of raw exam results, only 13 are effective when pupil background, prior ability and social context are allowed for (Table 10.2). Conversely, of the ineffective schools, only six are significantly below average on the adjusted results. In other words, 20 of the low-performing schools do "as well as could be expected" given their intake.

Table 10.3 presents the correlations between school residuals based on "raw" outcomes and those based on adjustments for pupil background, ability and social context. The two sets of residuals are significantly related, with particularly high values for measures of personal/social development.[1] It is clear, however, that the two residuals for Junior Cert exam performance are far from being perfectly correlated, indicating the problems with basing an assessment of schools on raw exam results alone.

TABLE 10.3: CORRELATIONS BETWEEN RAW AND ADJUSTED SCHOOL RESIDUALS AT JUNIOR CERT

Pupil outcome	*Pearson's correlation*
Junior Cert Grade Point Average	0.46*
Absenteeism	0.83*
Potential drop-out	0.58*
Stress	0.68*
Academic self-image	0.83*
Locus of control	0.93*
Body image	0.80*

Note: * significant at the <.05 level.

In addition, the imprecision associated with the detailed ranking of schools in terms of their effectiveness must be recognised. Figure 10.1 presents 95 per cent confidence intervals for adjusted school-level residuals for Junior Cert exam performance (see Goldstein and Healy, 1995). It is clear that the intervals for individual schools overlap considerably and that only the "top" and "bottom" schools can be clearly distinguished.

---

[1] The importance of these values should not be over-estimated, however, since only a small number of schools are significantly different from the average for these measures (see Table 10.1).

FIGURE 10.1: CONFIDENCE INTERVALS FOR ADJUSTED SCHOOL
RESIDUALS — JUNIOR CERT PERFORMANCE

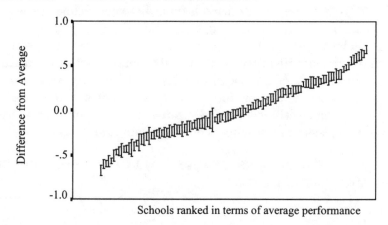

The relationship between different pupil outcomes has been
discussed in Chapter 9. An analysis of outlier schools indicates
that only a minority of schools are consistently "effective" (or "ineffective") across a range of outcomes. Adjusting for differences in
pupil intake, only six schools can be identified as effective on two
or more pupil outcomes while six schools can be identified as
ineffective on two or more outcomes.

10.2 LEAVING CERTIFICATE

Analyses of outlier schools at Leaving Cert level indicates greater
variation between schools in relation to exam performance than
measures of personal/social development (see Table 10.4). When
differences in pupil intake are taken into account, fewer schools
appear to differ significantly from the average. Controlling for
pupil background, prior performance and social context, 11 schools
are found to have significantly above average Leaving Cert results
with 17 schools having significantly below average results.

TABLE 10.4: NUMBER OF OUTLIER SCHOOLS BY OUTCOMES AMONG LEAVING CERT PUPILS

	"Raw"		Adjusted for pupil background		Adjusted for pupil background + JC results		Adjusted for background, JC results + social context	
	E	I	E	I	E	I	E	I
Leaving Cert GPAV	33	30	27	25	17	17	11	17
Stress	7	15	4	2	3	2	3	2
Academic self-image	5	3	2	3	7	13	6	11
Locus of control	1	0	1	0	2	0	2	0
Body image	9	11	1	4	1	3	1	2
Total number of schools	111		111		111		111	

There is greater difference between raw and adjusted results at Leaving Cert than at Junior Cert level, especially for exam performance (see Table 10.5). In addition, the ranking of schools changes substantially when pupil composition is taken into account.

TABLE 10.5: CORRELATIONS BETWEEN RAW AND ADJUSTED SCHOOL RESIDUALS AT LEAVING CERT

Pupil outcome	Pearson's correlation
Leaving Cert Grade Point Average	0.13
Stress	0.74*
Academic self-image	0.82*
Locus of control	0.97*
Body image	0.92*

Note: * significant at the <.05 level.

FIGURE 10.2: CONFIDENCE INTERVALS FOR ADJUSTED SCHOOL
RESIDUALS LEAVING CERT PERFORMANCE

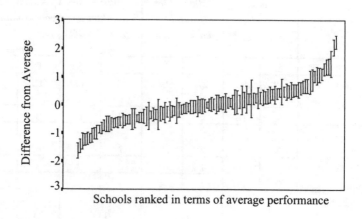

Figure 10.2 indicates that, as at Junior Cert, detailed rankings of schools cannot be regarded as precise.

In common with the Junior Cert level, schools are rarely consistently effective across the range of pupil outcomes. Controlling for pupil intake, only four schools are effective, and five ineffective, on two or more pupil outcomes.

10.3 RELATIONSHIP BETWEEN JUNIOR AND LEAVING CERTIFICATE RESULTS

Table 10.6 indicates the relationship between school-level residuals at Junior and Leaving Cert level. Residuals based on raw Leaving Cert outcomes are significantly related to those based on raw Junior Cert outcomes. For example, schools that have higher than average Leaving Cert exam results tend to have higher than average Junior Cert results (r = 0.77). Adjusted residuals are less highly correlated than raw residuals, that is, some of the correlation between Junior and Leaving Cert results reflects a similar pupil mix at both stages rather than a "school effect" *per se*.

TABLE 10.6: CORRELATIONS BETWEEN JUNIOR AND LEAVING CERT RESIDUALS

Pupil outcome	Raw residuals	Adjusted residuals
Exam performance	0.77*	0.22*
Stress	0.63*	0.32*
Academic self-image	0.36*	0.17
Locus of control	0.30*	0.28*
Body image	0.55*	0.23*

Note: * significant at the <.05 level.

Table 10.7 indicates the relationship between Junior and Leaving Cert outliers for exam performance. There is very little consistency between residuals at Leaving Cert and residuals at Junior Cert, once allowance is made for pupil intake. This lack of consistency reflects the fact that "effective" schools at Leaving Cert are those which promote academic progress, controlling for initial Junior Cert results. Consequently, it is possible for schools to have very low Junior Cert results (and be identified as "ineffective") but for pupils to make higher than average progress over the senior cycle (and be identified as "effective"). It is evident therefore that, unless account is taken of both the junior and senior cycles, effectiveness must be regarded as specific to a particular level.

TABLE 10.7: SCHOOL OUTLIERS FOR EXAM PERFORMANCE

Leaving Cert residuals	Junior Cert residuals		
	Effective	Average	Ineffective
Effective	2	7	2
Average	14	51	10
Ineffective	5	9	3
Total	21	67	15

10.4 CONCLUSIONS

Analyses in this chapter indicate the need for caution in the identification of "effective" or "ineffective" schools (see Goldstein and Spiegelhalter, 1996). In particular, detailed rankings of schools along one or more dimensions of effectiveness must be regarded as imprecise. In addition, schools are rarely consistently effective (or ineffective) across a range of pupil outcomes and across both the junior and senior cycles.

An examination of the features of outlier schools can, however, highlight some of the factors associated with enhanced (or reduced) pupil outcomes. The following chapter presents case-study material on four outlier and two "average" schools in order to detail school organisation and process "on the ground". Since less effective schools may be very different in character to more effective schools, it is important to include both types of school in the analysis.

Chapter 11

SCHOOL ORGANISATION AND PROCESS IN PRACTICE

11.1 INTRODUCTION

Chapter 10 has presented background information on "outlier" schools, that is, schools that are significantly different from the average in terms of one or more pupil outcomes. This information was used to select six schools which could be deemed "more academically effective", "average" and "less academically effective". These six schools were followed up in order to collect more detailed information on school organisation and process. In early 1997, school principals, vice-principals and teachers were interviewed on current practice in the school and on changes that had taken place since the original survey of pupils in 1994. Criteria, such as school sector, size, pupil mix and urban/rural location, were used in addition to academic progress[1] in the selection of these case-study schools (see Chapter 2).

As Chapter 10 has indicated, schools may not be equally "effective" on a range of pupil outcomes. One of the selected schools had consistently above average pupil progress at Junior and Leaving Certificate levels, low absenteeism and drop-out rates along with relatively low stress levels and average to high measures of personal-social development among pupils. The second "more academically effective" school had very high pupil progress at Junior Cert level with average progress at senior cycle, low drop-out rates, average levels of absenteeism and average measures of personal-social development. In the two "less academically effective" schools, academic progress was below average at Junior and Leaving Cert levels, absenteeism rates were average to high with fairly high levels of drop-out, average to

---

[1] In addition, data on pupil exam performance in 1996 were examined to ensure stability over time.

high stress levels and relatively low scores on measures of personal-social development. The two "average" schools tended to be "average" across a range of pupil outcomes, both academic and non-academic.

The remainder of this chapter considers school management and organisational practices and their relationship with pupil outcomes in the six schools.

11.2 PUPIL INTAKE

Three of the case-study schools are relatively comprehensive in their pupil intake while the other three schools have suffered from "cream-off" or cater for a more disadvantaged local area. School 5 is non-selective in its intake: "all the boys from the area come here" (Principal). School 1 is relatively comprehensive in its intake, although there may be some cream-off to a local fee-paying school. School 6 is similarly comprehensive in its intake but more recently another school in the area has been attempting to "cream-off" higher ability pupils. School 3 previously suffered "a great deal" from cream-off but the principal and vice-principal maintain that this has changed in recent years due to the school's emphasis on the provision of practical subjects and remedial education. School 2 takes most of its pupils from the "immediate area" (Principal) and the ethos of the school is to take all children who apply for entry. The vice-principal reports that in recent years, other schools have been creaming-off the higher ability pupils:

> We are losing the social mix and getting the lowest ability. There is a pecking order within the area. (Vice-principal, school 2)

School 4 is located in an area with a number of second-level schools. Traditionally, the school has "catered for students coming from the lower socio-economic groups, students with difficulties or remedial problems" (Principal), a pattern that seems to have intensified with the recent contraction in pupil numbers.

This pattern of school cream-off is reflected in the perceived incidence of literacy and numeracy problems among the first year intake. Perceived problems are less frequent in schools with more comprehensive intakes (schools 1, 5 and 6) with teachers estimating that approximately 13 to 15 per cent[2] of their intake have serious literacy or numeracy problems. In schools 2, 3 and 4, the reported incidence is significantly higher, ranging from 36 to 46 per cent of the first year intake.

Data from the pupil survey also indicate a difference between the six schools in their social mix. Pupils from schools 2, 3 and 4 were more likely than those from other schools to come from semi-skilled or unskilled manual backgrounds, to have unemployed parents and parents with lower levels of education.

In terms of academic performance, the "more effective" schools tend to have lower levels of literacy/numeracy problems while the "less effective" schools tend to have higher levels of such problems. It should be noted that the less effective schools show lower levels of academic progress among pupils even when differences in pupil background (including prior ability) are controlled for. Furthermore, a relatively high proportion of pupils in one of the "effective" schools come from semi-/unskilled manual backgrounds (although in overall terms the school is mixed socially) and these pupils have disproportionately high levels of parental unemployment compared with the national population. Similarly, schools 2, 3 and 4 are fairly similar in terms of pupil mix but pupils in school 2 have average, rather than lower, levels of academic progress.

11.3 EDUCATIONAL PHILOSOPHY

School management and teachers were questioned about the educational philosophy and objectives within the school. In general, staff feel they are addressing a set of complex and often diverse objectives. Very few stress academic success alone although it is argued that "there is a big emphasis on sending out everyone with the Leaving Cert" (Vice-principal, school 3). More frequently, an emphasis is placed on promoting the overall development of the pupil, both academic and non-academic:

> Our aim is to develop the full potential of all our students. We strive for academic excellence along with the spiritual, moral and social development of each student. (School brochure, school 6)

---

[2] This refers to the average pattern. It should be noted that there may be considerable differences within schools in the reported incidence of literacy/numeracy problems.

The philosophy or the objectives in the school is to provide a caring atmosphere in which we can help children to develop all their functions, social, emotional, intellectual, physical, in so far as we can provide an atmosphere in which that can all flourish and develop. (Principal, school 1)

[The objective is] to provide an education suitable to their abilities, to enable them to reach their potential and direct them to the area of work or study that they are best suited to. (Vice-principal, school 5)

Two of the schools, in particular, see their orientation as being towards more disadvantaged students, although operating in terms of a non-selective entrance policy:

We're for the education of all children which means that we take all the children who apply to us and that covers a range of abilities from the very bright to the extremely weak and also a range of family backgrounds in terms of the area. (Principal, school 2)

Our philosophy is very much inclusive of the most excluded and marginalised. (Vice-principal, school 2)

[We] have . . . students drawn from a variety of backgrounds but with a strong emphasis of socially disadvantaged students. (Vice-principal, school 4)

This orientation is linked to the need to provide an appropriate curriculum to meet the needs of these students:

We must provide relevant provision for all the different people which involves taking on all the different courses and operating sometimes with smaller numbers in classes because of the various needs of the children. (Principal, school 2)

Retention of students throughout the senior cycle is itself a goal [as is] providing a curriculum that responds to the diversity of needs so, for instance, we've introduced Leaving Cert Applied for the weaker students at senior cycle. (Vice-principal, school 4)

In addition, three of the schools see their philosophy as encompassing groups outside the traditional second-level sector, including post-Leaving Certificate students and adults.

There is no clear relationship between focusing on academic outcomes as a school objective and actual levels of academic performance within the school; there is no significant difference between teachers in the more academically effective schools and others in the proportion mentioning academic goals or objectives. However, teachers in the less effective schools are somewhat less likely to mention the full development of the pupil as a goal within the school. Objectives also vary according to the type of pupils in the school, with staff in the two girls' schools more frequently mentioning the importance of social/emotional development than those in the other schools.

11.4 CURRICULAR PROVISION AND SUBJECT CHOICE

All of the six schools had modified their curriculum over the three years since the previous survey. Three of the schools had introduced Technology while two schools had introduced German as a second language. In general, school management tends to be satisfied with subject provision at junior and senior cycle, although in one school which provides a wide range of subjects, the principal remarks that "the curriculum is over-loaded at the moment" (school 1). This view is echoed by the vice-principal who remarks that:

> There is nearly too much choice. It can be a menace. Some don't know their own mind. It can be based on the personality of the teacher. Their motivation is questionable. A lot of pupils change subjects. (School 1)

The majority of teachers in the six schools feel that "there is a good range of subjects on offer to pupils". Satisfaction with the range of subjects provided is highest in school 1, which is the largest school with the widest range of subjects, and lowest in school 2 which has the narrowest range of subjects. A number of staff have expressed concern about the difficulty of maintaining curricular provision in the context of declining pupil numbers:

> The problem of falling numbers leads to difficulty in keeping subject choices. (Teacher, school 6)

> The problems of shrinking numbers means limited subject
> choice and problems for time-tabling. (Teacher, school 6)

More and less effective schools do not vary substantially from
each other in terms of teacher satisfaction with subject provision.

There is no clear-cut relationship between school effectiveness
and perceived cleanliness of the school building or adequacy of
school facilities. Teachers in school 2 are most likely to report that
the building is always kept clean and tidy. However, a substantial
minority (one-third) of teachers in one of the more effective
schools (school 6) feel this is not the case. Satisfaction with facilities is highest in one of the less effective schools (school 3) with
the two more effective schools showing fairly high levels of
dissatisfaction with facilities. Management in four of the schools
expressed dissatisfaction with sports and PE facilities while three
schools have inadequate resources for practical/technical subjects.

11.4.1 Subject choice at junior cycle

Chapters 4 and 5 indicate that, on average, greater flexibility in
subject choice at junior and senior cycle is associated with improved academic performance among pupils, all else being equal.
However, more detailed examination of the case-study schools
indicates that schools may vary significantly in the way in which
subjects and subject levels are made available to pupils.

Pupils in schools 5, 6 and 2 choose their Junior Cert subjects at
the end of first year. Subject choice is more flexible in school 6
where pupils take five core subjects and have a free choice of four
from a list of eight subjects. Previously choice was more limited
with seven core exam subjects and only two optional subjects.[3]
Choice of Junior Cert subjects is relatively limited in school 5;
pupils take seven core exam subjects and select two out of four
subjects, three of which are technical/practical subjects. In school
2, pupils in the top two classes take seven core subjects with one
optional subject while pupils in the bottom two classes take eight
core subjects (see below).

Pupils in schools 1 and 3 have a "sampling" system prior to
subject choice. In school 1 pupils try every subject for the first
week; previously this occurred for the first two months but "we

---

[3] It should be noted that the data on Junior Cert exam performance used in
the above analyses relate to a period when this more restricted choice was
in operation.

found they were making their choices on who else was in the class and what teacher there was rather than on the subject, whether the subject was good for them or not" (Principal). Pupils take five core subjects and choose four options. However, the degree of choice available may be somewhat illusory as, due to numbers, a lottery system is used for access to some practical subjects. School 3 has recently introduced a system for first years whereby they make their choice having had "six weeks of everything" (Vice-Principal).

> The school is trying to offer as wide a range of subjects as possible, especially to cater for weaker pupils. In first year, they get to try all the subjects for a few weeks. [This is] working well [and has made a] difference for non-traditional subjects; quite a number of boys are taking Home Economics. (Teacher, school 3)

School 4 has the least flexible approach to subject choice. Pupils choose their subjects in May before entry but there is some lee-way for subsequent change in the first term. They previously had a sampling system for the whole of first year "but it just didn't work" (Principal). Core and optional subjects depend on which class pupils are in. Those in the top two classes take five core subjects and choose three optional subjects. The bottom two classes do six core subjects with two optional subjects.

The two more academically effective schools appear to encourage the take-up of higher level courses by postponing choice until March of the exam year: "I try to encourage that that choice be made as late as possible in Junior Cert" (Principal, School 6). In the latter case, access to higher level is decided on the basis of "negotiation rather than teacher recommendation in as much as the teacher doesn't have the final say, the pupil will make the final decision" (Principal, school 6). However, there is likely to be some prior selection of pupils as these schools use setting for Irish, English and Maths in third year. Pupils in school 1 make their final decision about subject levels around Easter of the exam year although pupils are graded by the school at the end of first year as a basis for allocation to set classes.

School 4 shares a similar emphasis on promoting the take-up of higher level courses: "we go up to the wire [in terms of choosing levels], as late as we can get away with it in terms of the Department . . . I like to encourage as many to take higher level as possible" (Vice-principal) though this flexibility would seem to be limited by the practice of streaming in the school. Similarly, the use of streaming in schools 2 and 3 can restrict access to higher level courses: "it is not always possible to do honours within a class, it depends on the good-will of the teacher" (Vice-principal, school 3).

In summary, the positive impact of "flexibility" in subject choice appears to relate only to the postponement of subject choice rather than to the number and type of optional subjects available to pupils. There is a tension for schools between facilitating as wide a choice as possible for pupils, providing a comprehensive cur-riculum for pupils (in order to maximise subsequent educational and career options) and having adequate staffing/resources to do so. Among the case-study schools, the more academically effective schools appear to be ones where choices about subject levels are delayed as long as possible.

11.4.2 Subject choice at senior cycle

In general, flexibility in subject choice is more evident at Leaving Cert level. In five of the schools, pupils are first given an open choice before optional packages are constructed:

> We go out of our way as much as possible to try and facili-tate what the students want. (Principal, school 5)

> Pupils are given a list of options and it's on that then that we make the subject choices for next year. Some students won't get all the subjects they want but they have a major input. (Principal, school 4)

All of the schools mention the need for "continuity" in subject take-up (for example, taking Science at Junior Cert level in order to take Chemistry at Leaving Cert level). However, the principal in school 5 stresses that are "no hard and fast rules" regarding conditions for taking specific subjects.

In three of the schools, pupils choose their subject levels for the Leaving Cert around February or March of the exam year:

> This is an on-going process which would have its final phase on the basis of the results of the Mocks. (Principal, school 6)

However, in other cases subject levels in core subjects have to be selected "pretty fast" (Principal, school 1) because of setting and in schools 3 and 4 access to higher level courses is influenced by class allocation.

In summary, as at Junior Cert level the more academically effective schools tend to allow greater flexibility to their pupils in the timing of choice of subjects and subject levels for the Leaving Cert.

11.4.3 New curricular programmes

The introduction of new programmes within the schools reflected two factors: first, a desire to provide more appropriate curricula for certain groups of pupils, particularly lower ability pupils; and second, the need to diversify provision in the face of declining pupil numbers. School 2, in particular, emphasises the need to provide relevant curricula to their pupils; to this end, they have introduced the Junior Cert Schools Programme, the Leaving Cert Applied Programme and Transition Year. Due to declining pupil numbers and increasing cream-off, the two less academically effective schools have adopted an explicit policy of expanding Post-Leaving Cert provision, although this process has tended to take place in parallel with the introduction of new programmes (such as the Leaving Cert Applied Programme and the Leaving Cert Vocational Programme) within the second-level part of the school. In contrast, the two more academically effective schools have not yet introduced new second-level programmes (except for Transition Year), concentrating on integrating all pupils into the "mainstream". This approach is facilitated by a more comprehensive pupil intake.

In general, teachers are positive about the introduction of the new second-level courses, stressing that curricula are now more appropriate to their pupil intake and are likely to result in a reduction in pupil drop-out:

> The introduction of Transition Year and Leaving Cert Applied has been very positive for education in general. They accommodate students whose potential was not being developed, the marginalised. (Teacher, school 1)

> LCAP is keeping students who wouldn't do the Leaving Cert. (Teacher, school 1)

> With the new JCE and LCAP, we are hoping to keep 68 to 70 out of 70 first years. Very few of the current Junior

> Certs intend to leave. Before we were losing quite a few
> out of Junior Cert. . . . This [the introduction of new
> programmes] reflects the school is catering for the needs of
> the kids we have. (Teacher, school 2)

> In LCAP and JCE, they are working more at their own
> pace and taking responsibility. (Teacher, school 2)

> LCAP is very positive; it has given a structure to children
> who would not have survived in the traditional Leaving
> Cert. (Teacher, school 4)

All of the schools have provided or are providing Transition Year
to pupils. In five of the schools, access to Transition Year is based
on student self-selection, although in many cases school management would veto pupils who were likely to be disruptive. One of
the more academically effective schools has made Transition Year
compulsory for all pupils. This approach has been considered by
other schools:

> We would like to put Transition Year as obligatory. But the
> attitude of the students is that when they reach that age
> they want to be able to get out as quick as they can. So if
> we put it obligatory, we feel that the actual idea of them
> sitting their Leaving Cert . . . would be sacrificed. (Princi-
> pal, school 4)

Indeed, in the case of school 5 an obligatory Transition Year has
caused some operational problems in terms of student motivation,
especially on the part of more academic pupils, and parental resis-
tance to the concept:

> There's a very, very poor perception out there amongst the
> parents about the relevance of Transition Year. It saddens
> me when I hear from parents "Look, all I want from my
> young fella is X number of points, that's all I want".
> (Principal, school 5)

School management in the six schools tends to stress fairly similar objectives in relation to Transition Year provision, including
maturity, "personal development of the student" (Principal, school
4), "developing social skills" (Principal, school 5), "widening the
scope of learning opportunities" (Principal, school 6), and "to

enable students . . . to make more informed choices in fifth year" (Vice-principal, school 5). School management are broadly satisfied with the operation of Transition Year in their school:

> We've seen the effect on the first group that we had, they're in fifth year now and they're very motivated to work and have certainly matured. (Principal, school 2)

> [Those who take TY] definitely do better in fifth and sixth year. Those who don't do it miss out socially, in interacting with their peers, to be able to work with other people, and in setting and achieving goals. (Vice-Principal, school 6)

However, two of the less academically effective schools are phasing out Transition Year in order to provide the Leaving Cert Applied programme. It is considered that this programme will be more appropriate to the needs of their pupils and reflects the fact that:

> The students more or less told us they would not do three years for a Leaving Cert. (Principal, school 4)

In contrast, school 2 (with a similar pupil mix) provides Transition Year on an optional basis while at the same time providing LCAP.

In summary, the case of school 2 indicates the importance of curricular adaptation and flexibility in securing better academic results with a more disadvantaged pupil intake. While the less academically effective schools have also introduced new curricular programmes, this has taken place in the context of a shift in focus away from traditional second-level provision to cater for non-traditional student groups (such as PLC students and adults). In contrast, the two more academically effective schools have tended to integrate lower ability pupils into the mainstream Junior and Leaving Cert programmes. Consequently, it appears that curricular adaptation is not a necessary condition of academic progress but may potentially serve as a route to academic improvement for schools catering for more disadvantaged pupil intakes.

11.5 CLASS ALLOCATION

Chapters 4 and 5 have indicated the negative effect of streaming on pupil performance, particularly for those allocated to the bottom/remedial class. However, a closer examination of the six schools indicates that there is some variation from this general relationship. Among the six case-study schools, three use streaming and three mixed ability in structuring base classes at junior cycle. The two schools with higher academic performance use mixed ability[4] while those with lower academic performance use streaming. Of the two "average" schools, one uses streaming and one uses mixed ability base classes at junior cycle. In general, schools are less likely to use streaming, and more likely to use mixed ability base classes with setting in particular subjects (usually Irish, English and/or Maths), at Leaving Cert level because of greater subject choice and some differentiation due to new programmes such as LCAP and LCVP. Two of the schools continue to use streaming at senior cycle while the extent to which setting is used varies among the other schools.

Three sets of reasons have been presented for using streaming rather than mixed ability allocation. First, it is argued that classroom teaching is impracticable when the class is mixed ability:

> We felt because we have such a huge range of abilities, from very bright down to remedial, that we just felt by putting them into the particular groups, it was easier to actually manage it. (Principal, school 4)

> You need training and you need resources to make it [mixed ability] work. And the spread is quite broad, you have some children coming in who have only bare literacy and others quite good. So we haven't found it worked, the pure mixed ability. (Vice-principal, school 4)

> It [streaming] gives a brilliant child an opportunity and special treatment for lower ability pupils. (Principal, school 3)

> In relation to the Junior Cert . . . it's absolutely impossible to have the children mixed in a class, where you'd have honours and ordinary level and foundation level. No teacher could take that on board. (Principal, school 2)

---

[4] Both schools had moved from a system of streaming to one of mixed ability.

Second, it is argued that mixed ability teaching tends to be particularly detrimental to higher ability pupils:

> The requirements to maximise the potential of bright students make it [streaming] necessary. (Principal, school 3)

Unusually, school 2 explicitly adopted streaming in order to facilitate progress among lower ability (as well as higher ability) pupils:

> We came back to the streaming about three years ago because on an overall evaluation of what was happening in mixed ability, we felt that the weaker children were really lost, weren't able to be given the attention within the group and the brighter children were also missing out. The group that were holding their own were the middle group because what was happening was that the teacher was aiming at a middle ground in terms of the standard of work that they were presenting and requiring back from the students. . . . And we felt that we were in a much better position [with streaming] than we had been in the previous year, that the kids were much happier and performing much better at their own level. (Principal, school 2)

However, it is recognised that streaming can have negative effects in terms of pupil motivation, self-esteem and drop-out:

> Moving to mixed ability, there would be social advantages, there would be advantages in terms of self-esteem with the mixing of the students. (Vice-principal, school 4)

> One disadvantage is that by third year the remedial class is down to nine or even two because of high drop-out. It's demoralising for teachers to have such a small class. By third year there is a loss of interest among both pupils and teachers. (Vice-principal, school 3)

Staff in schools which use mixed ability base classes have also expressed some reluctance about introducing "pure" mixed ability teaching. However, in these schools these issues have been resolved by using setting for a number of subjects:

> I think that in Leaving Cert . . . it's very, very difficult to teach higher level and ordinary level together, given the

> present structure of the programme. . . . In English, for
> example, where you've to cover more material for taking
> the higher level paper, well it's almost impossible to teach
> that in a mixed situation. (Principal, school 6)

Other staff stress the advantages of mixed ability allocation:

> I think there's a very distinct advantage [in mixed ability]
> because the people who were separated out as being
> remedial children . . . their self-esteem in the school was
> low, discipline would usually be a problem and I would
> definitely be in favour of the non-streaming system we
> have here in that they're in with their peers and they're
> working to the best of their ability. . . . Being present with
> the better students as well gives them that extra incentive
> . . . there's a better class environment having the mixed
> ability. (Principal, school 5)

> We'd debated it over and over again. We did have stream-
> ing and we found that the weaker children felt very
> branded and it was a big burden on them even though
> they couldn't be in the honours class. (Principal, school 1)

11.6 REMEDIAL PROVISION

All of the schools provide extra support for pupils with learning
difficulties, although schools vary in the availability of resources,
the type of system used and in the number of pupils in need of
(and receiving) such support. Even in schools where lower ability
pupils are grouped into separate base classes, schools tend to
withdraw pupils from certain lessons for extra assistance on a
small group or individual basis. School 2 appears to have a more
intensive approach to remedial support, allowing for fourteen to
fifteen class periods per week:

> Pupils are withdrawn, usually in small groups and in
> extreme cases as individuals. But the teacher feels
> obviously she can reach more of them if they're in small
> groups because so many of them need the learning sup-
> port. (Principal, school 2)

School 4 uses a withdrawal system for Maths but provides a
second class-room teacher for remedial English classes. In all

schools, provision tends to be targeted at those in the junior cycle, particularly first years:

> Emphasis is placed on first year. Whatever remaining time is left, it is distributed among the other years. I try to work with those most needing help. (Remedial teacher, school 2)

Schools vary significantly in the proportion of first years receiving such help, ranging from 10 per cent in school 5 to 60 per cent in school 4, a pattern mirroring the reported incidence in literacy/numeracy problems (see above). In addition, extra support tends to be provided in English rather than in other subjects, such as Maths (with the exception of school 4).

Most of the remedial teachers consider remedial provision in their school to be successful (at least for those pupils who currently receive help):

> Feedback from other teachers indicates it has been successful. Retesting on various tests indicates great improvements in pupils. (Remedial teacher, school 6)

However, a number of issues have been raised by remedial teachers. First, staff feel there is a need to cover pupils throughout their second-level careers and to provide support to a greater number of pupils:

> Beyond first year, it [provision] is less successful. It is not available across the board in later years and often time for one-to-one is unavailable. (Remedial teacher, school 2)

> Eighteen to twenty per cent of the school need help but not all are getting enough. (Remedial teacher, school 1)

> We need to maintain provision that is provided in first year throughout second, third, fifth and sixth year. (Remedial teacher, school 2)

> Not all pupils who need remedial are getting it; there is only adequate provision for first years. (Remedial teacher, school 6)

Second, it is considered that provision should not be confined to English:

> A remedial Maths teacher is urgently needed. (Remedial teacher, school 2)

> The Maths side can be lost out on. (Teacher, school 5)

Third, a number stress the need for extra teaching resources on an ex-quota basis:

> We need another remedial teacher. (Remedial teacher, school 1)

> More pupils should get help; there's only one remedial teacher. (Teacher, school 1)

There does not appear to be any clear relationship between the proportion of pupils needing such assistance and the current level of provision to the six case-study schools in terms of teachers and teaching hours. This would appear to indicate the necessity of more detailed assessments of school needs in the allocation of resources for remedial provision.

11.7 DISCIPLINARY CLIMATE

All of the schools have a written set of rules which is given to pupils and parents and (with the exception of school 3) signed by parents:

> [The rules] are actually on the front page of the school journal. And they then become signed by the parents as an acknowledgement of agreement and parents sign this page every week. So it's a kind of means of communication between home and school really. (Principal, school 6)

While schools differ in their specific rules, all of the disciplinary codes are underpinned by the wish to promote respect within the school and to provide an environment which facilitates learning:

> I believe very strongly that students have a right to learn, they have a right to have the required discipline in the class to enable that to happen. And if there are people present who are showing disrespect or are abusive to

teachers, I think, taking the rights of the students into account, it is important that they are dealt with very, very firmly. (Principal, school 5)

The school rules are based on respect, respect for themselves, respect for other pupils and for staff and the property of the place. (Principal, school 1)

We encourage a basic respect between all the different groups that are involved in school-life: teachers, pupils, parents, ancillary staff. And we feel if every group has that right that other things follow, that you don't have as much indiscipline or boldness. (Principal, school 2)

Schools differ, however, in the formal procedures adopted for disciplinary issues and the extent to which these procedures are backed up by sanctions. School 5 uses a year head system, with more serious problems referred upwards to the principal:

The teacher deals with the problem first of all in the class; then, if that doesn't work, the teacher passes it on to the year teacher and the year teacher would talk and advise. If that doesn't work, then it would go back to the year teacher again and the year teacher would put them on report and at that stage the parents would be informed. Then they would come to me; then at that stage they would be suspended. (Principal, school 5)

Other schools use a class tutor system as the first point of intervention:

What we try to encourage is that every subject teacher at his or her own level deals with the discipline to begin with ... but then after that if they find that the student is difficult, they pass them on to the class tutor. And if the class tutor finds that they're not responding, they are then passed on to the year head. (Principal, school 2)

First of all, the teacher in the class or in the corridor [deals with discipline]. They might go to the tutor and that might finish it. If it persisted and the tutor was getting nowhere, they would go to the year head. And if that persisted or if it became a very inflammatory thing all of a

> sudden, it would come to the vice-principal and myself.
> (Principal, school 1)

However, there can be variation within the school in how the disciplinary system is implemented:

> Some teachers work through the system, others don't
> bother at all, they just send them straight in here.
> (Principal, school 1)

Some teachers mention the need for a more consistent approach to discipline within the school, "implementing rules and regulations across the board" (Teacher, school 1), with "clearer rules" (Teacher, school 1) and a "need to be standardised in discipline" (Teacher, school 1).

In four of the schools, pupil behaviour is monitored through record or progress sheets:

> We use a progress sheet for people who are disrupting
> classes, not behaving in class and the progress sheet has
> to be signed at the end of every class by the teacher. And
> at the end of the day they have to bring it home and get it
> signed by their parents which means that the parents
> have to read that this person was very talkative in such a
> class or had no homework. (Principal, school 1)

> If a child violates badly some section of the school rules,
> that is recorded in a record book which is kept in the
> office. And if a child has three entries in that record book,
> they get a warning letter home to their parents and if they
> have another entry, they appear before the discipline
> committee with their parents. And that may result in
> suspension or in detention . . . depending on the nature of
> it. (Principal, school 2)

Punctuality is also monitored through a "late book" system in three of the schools.

In the two more academically effective schools and in one of the "average" schools (school 2), disciplinary procedures involve parents at a fairly early stage:

> We have a late book system. . . . And if they're late,
> immediately a letter goes home which I find very effective

> because parents like it and they respond to it. (Principal, school 5)

> Notes for absences and notes of homework [in the homework journal], all these kind of notes are passed between home and class mistress generally or I would write in them fairly regularly myself if there's somebody out of order. (Principal, school 6)

A number of teachers stress the need for adequate support for schools in dealing with disciplinary issues:

> A code of practice in relation to discipline is needed nationally. (Teacher, school 5)

> Discipline has declined and become a problem because there is no overall policy from the Department. (Teacher, school 5)

> The government should bring out a policy on discipline. Management and teachers' hands are tied. (Teacher, school 6)

Staff management and teachers were questioned about the frequency of discipline problems, including pupils' talking in class, failing to do homework, lack of punctuality, absenteeism, damaging school property, bullying and being abusive to teachers. There are significant differences between the schools in the reported frequency of such problems. Discipline problems are less frequently reported in the more academically effective schools[5] and more frequently reported in the average and less academically effective schools:

> Discipline in the classroom is a problem. It's taking teacher attention and time; it's affecting children who want to learn. (Teacher, school 4)

---

[5] A scale of reported discipline problems (with an alpha value is 0.81) was derived from the teachers' questionnaires. Inter-school variation in reported discipline problems is statistically significant.

In addition, teachers in the more effective schools have more positive views of pupil behaviour with the vast majority reporting that "nearly all" pupils are well-behaved within the school; this is reported by four-fifths of the teachers in school 6 and two-thirds of those in school 5. Teachers in schools 1 and 4 have the least positive reports (with a substantial minority of teachers in school 4 reporting that less than half of the pupils are well-behaved). This difference is also evident in relation to reports of pupils' behaviour in the grounds of the school. A similar pattern is found in relation to reported respect for teachers with a clear difference between the more effective schools and others.

In summary, the more academically effective schools appear to be ones which have succeeded in creating an orderly learning environment for pupils (see Scheerens and Bosker, 1997, for similar findings internationally). This has been achieved through a consistent application of school rules and procedures along with relatively early involvement of parents in disciplinary procedures. It is not intended to imply that some schools do not face serious discipline issues which are not of their making. However, inadequate or inconsistent responses to breaches in discipline may result in a "vicious cycle" of disimprovement whereby a disorderly school environment has a negative effect on pupil performance and disaffected pupils may in turn cause greater classroom disruption.

11.8 HOMEWORK POLICY

Interviews with school management indicate a degree of teacher autonomy in relation to homework policy within the school:

> Teachers have freedom in setting and checking homework.
> (Vice-principal, school 5)

However, a number of staff stress the emphasis placed on homework within the school:

> Obviously every teacher knows the worth of homework. And I notice several notes going home to say that homework hasn't been done . . . so there is a strict eye. (Principal, school 6)

In some cases, there are formal procedures for students rather than teachers:

> Homework is to be done and handed up on the required day. It's to be written into the homework journal. (Vice-principal, school 6)

> If they consistently fail to do it [homework], that's where . . . the year head would be brought in. Their parents would be consulted on it. (Principal, school 4)

> There is a homework notebook. As tutor, your role is to check this, especially in the junior years. (Teacher, school 1)

> There is a duplicate book with a list of pupils who don't do their homework. After three occasions, this is followed up by the year heads. (Teacher, school 1)

However, two of the less academically effective schools report difficulties in implementing the formal procedures for students, difficulties which appear to relate to inconsistency in applying homework rules:

> Most, 75 per cent, [of the homework diaries] are signed by the parents but I don't think they're checked. They're useful in times of crisis but it's too difficult with a lot of pupils. (Vice-principal, school 3)

> The biggest single problem we have is trying to get students to do their homework. A lot of them, particularly at the weaker end of each year, don't do it. . . . Some teachers would be very insistent on it and others wouldn't. (Principal, school 4)

> Teachers have different approaches to the giving of homework. And more importantly, they give different types of homework, depending on the level of students. So one of my main problems is getting a certain amount of homework given to weaker students. What can happen is teachers can stop giving homework to students who don't do great homework and loading it on for others. (Vice-principal, school 4)

It is interesting to note the variation within schools in the way teachers characterise homework policy. A significant minority of teachers in the six schools state there is no policy as such; however, this is the case for the majority of teachers in one of the less effective schools (school 3). Teachers in the more effective schools are more likely to report the existence of formal procedures for homework than those in other schools:

> There is a report system in operation. If pupils do no homework a few times, it goes to the year head. They can be put on report for a week. (Teacher, school 5)

> There is a journal system since September. Pupils have to write in their homework every day; it's signed by the tutor and parents. It's working well. Students know their journal will be seen. (Teacher, school 6)

School 2 also has relatively high reporting of formal procedures and/or rules.

> The subject teacher goes to the tutor who goes to the year head, if they don't do their homework. (Teacher, school 2)

> There is a homework journal and teachers are to ensure that homework is done. There are sanctions if it is not done: writing out homework three to five times, detention, contact with parents. (Teacher, school 2)

Teachers in the other schools sometimes report inconsistencies in the enforcement of existing homework procedures:

> The system is fairly loose at the moment; it's not always enforced or efficient. (Teacher, school 1)

> It [homework policy] is very vague: homework has to be done. There are no real sanctions. (Teacher, school 1)

> The homework notebook is checked at the tutor time in the morning. It is enforced in first year but tends to lapse after that. (Teacher, school 1)

> There is no overall agreement on the quality of homework and checking. (Teacher, school 4)

> Rules are not implemented by the majority of teachers. There is little follow-up when homework is not done. A note of failure to do homework may be noted in the journal, but it is rarely acted on by anyone. (Teacher, school 4)

The issue of a consistent approach to homework policy across the whole school has been stressed as a central element of academic effectiveness in the international literature (Scheerens and Bosker, 1997; Sammons *et al.*, 1997).

11.9 TEACHER EXPECTATIONS OF PUPIL PERFORMANCE

Chapters 4 to 6 indicated that teacher expectations (as reported by pupils) are positively associated with higher academic performance among pupils. The case-studies of the six schools allow us to explore expectations for pupils from the teacher perspective. School management and staff were asked what proportion of pupils they expected to stay on to the Leaving Cert, expected to go on to higher education, and expected to obtain at least one "honour" in their Junior and Leaving Cert exams.

School management in the more effective schools expects the vast majority of pupils coming into first year to stay on to the Leaving Cert. Teachers in these schools, along with those in school 1, report a higher average, and lower variation in responses around this average, of pupils expected to stay on to the Leaving Certificate. Conversely, the two less academically effective schools report the lowest staying rates:

> There used to be anything up to 25 to 30 per cent drop-out after Junior Cert but that didn't happen in the last couple of years. But we've noticed the trend is coming back . . . the problem is once the economic boom starts, they start to drop out again. (Principal, school 4)

School 2 more closely resembles the less effective schools in terms of this pattern than the other schools. However, it is considered that the introduction of new programmes into the curriculum will help to reduce pupil drop-out:

> The Leaving Cert Applied will definitely affect retention post-Junior Cert. The evidence is, even though we've only had it for one year, that we're holding students who would otherwise have dropped out because the weaker end of the senior cycle was probably causing most trouble in the secondary curriculum. (Vice-principal, school 4)

Expectations in relation to pupils achieving honours in the Junior or Leaving Cert follow a fairly similar pattern. Expectations are higher for pupils in schools 5, 6 and 1 (which are more comprehensive in intake), and lower for those in schools 2, 3 and 4 (which have a greater tendency to suffer from "cream-off"). In addition, staff in schools 5, 6 and 1 are more likely to report that they expect Leaving Cert pupils to go on to higher education. Expectations are particularly low in school 2 where it is reported that "there is no culture of getting the children into third-level" (Vice-principal).

The pattern of expectations found may reflect a realistic appraisal by teachers of pupil performance within the school or may operate as a "self-fulfilling prophecy" whereby pupils "live up" (or down) to these expectations. British research has indicated that there is a tendency by staff in less academically effective schools to "blame" the pupil intake for poor academic performance (Sammons *et al.*, 1997). The pattern found among the "average" case-study schools is interesting. School 1 has relatively high expectations among teachers but is "average" in terms of actual academic progress among pupils in the school. In contrast, teachers in school 2 have relatively low expectations (although expectations of performance are high on the part of the principal) but the school is average in terms of "value added" with a more disadvantaged
pupil intake than in school 1.

11.10 TEACHER PERCEPTIONS OF PUPILS

Teachers in the more effective schools are more likely than those in average or less effective schools to report that "nearly all" pupils enjoy school. Conversely, teachers in the less effective schools are more likely to report that "less than half" or "only a few" pupils enjoy school. Although dealing with a similar pupil intake, teachers in one of the "average" schools, school 2, are less likely than those in the less effective schools to report that only a minority of pupils enjoy school. School 1 shows a pattern between the more effective and the less effective schools.

Teachers in the more effective schools are somewhat more likely than others to report that "nearly all" pupils find schoolwork interesting, although only a minority (fewer than one-tenth) of all teachers report this. Most teachers in the less effective schools report that only a minority of pupils are interested in schoolwork. Average schools are somewhat closer to the pattern in less effective schools.

Teachers were asked whether pupils worked at a level appropriate to their abilities. Those in the more effective schools are less likely to report that only a minority of pupils work at an appropriate level. The pattern of responses in average and less effective schools overlaps with half of the teachers in the average schools reporting this compared with 39 per cent in school 4 and 32 per cent in school 3.

Teachers in the more effective schools are more likely to report that pupils experience success and achievement. School 2 has the lowest reported level.

The majority of teachers in the more effective schools report that "nearly all" pupils in the school show respect for teachers. Reported levels are lower in the average and less effective schools.

The above measures were combined into a scale "teacher perceptions of pupils" with an alpha value of 0.75. Between-school differences are found to be statistically significant with the most positive perceptions of pupils found in the more effective schools and little variation among the average and less effective schools.

11.11 FORMAL PASTORAL CARE STRUCTURES WITHIN THE SCHOOL

The level of development of pastoral care provision, the objectives of this provision and the extent to which it is underpinned by a positive informal culture varies from school to school. Among the case-study schools, school 2 appears to have the most developed approach to pastoral care with a strong emphasis on pupil support and personal/social development. There is a formal programme usually taught by class tutors and co-ordinated by the head of pastoral care. The programme is student-centred:

> What happens is the pastoral care co-ordinator meets with the people teaching the programme once a week and at that meeting they highlight the particular needs of their

> group at that particular time. And then the programme is planned around that so really the programme is in response to the needs of the students. (Principal, school 2)

> We develop the programme ourselves; we set the issues for each year group and deal with issues that would arise. (Pastoral care co-ordinator, school 2)

The objectives of this programme are:

> For the student to have a greater understanding of themselves and others; to build up confidence and self-esteem; how to cope with emotions and feelings; preparing for study skills. (Teacher, school 2)

In addition, a counsellor is available for pupils and parents; their role is:

> To help and personally counsel pupils in difficulty in terms of abuse, parental problems, relationships. I am a resource for staff; teachers can approach me for advice. I act as trainer for programmes, such as prefect training, the support system for first and fifth years, and train teachers. . . . I work with adults, including many parents, on personal development. (Counsellor, school 2)

School management are fairly satisfied with pastoral care provision in the school.

In the other schools, pastoral care tends to be organised through the class tutor or year head systems. However, this can lead to some tension between disciplinary and pastoral care roles:

> I would prefer if their [year heads'] duties would not just involve discipline, would not just involve role-calling or absenteeism, that they would take on some particular topic with first years, maybe the transition from primary into second-level, maybe in third year relationships, Transition Year, drugs. (Principal, school 5)

> My perception is that their [class tutors'] role is more disciplinary than pastoral. (Principal, school 6)

However, management in school 1 is satisfied that their class tutor system in conjunction with a pastoral care team provides adequate support to pupils.

Five of the schools provide some class time for personal development issues, although the focus and target groups differ between schools. Such programmes include health education, Relationships and Sexuality Education, "civics" and personal development for Transition Year. With the exception of school 2, these programmes are available only to a certain range of year groups and differ in the breadth of their focus. However, timetabling constraints can impact on the provision of formal programmes:

> The only way we could actually do better would be by having more personal development programmes in the curriculum but the time in the curriculum is being squeezed out. (Vice-principal, school 4)

With the exception of school 2, school management is happier that specific problems can be identified through the pastoral care structures rather than with the impact of these structures on general personal and social development among pupils. Interestingly, school management in the more academically effective schools is quite critical of current provision in their schools and is in the process of introducing new structures. The principal in school 5 is not satisfied that current provision is promoting personal/social development among pupils and targeting particular problems "could be very much hit and miss", being strongly reliant on the principal along with "some year teachers [who] are excellent at targeting and pinpointing a problem" (Principal). However, the pastoral care co-ordinator reports that "problems have been successfully dealt with, nipped in the bud". In school 6, the principal sees provision as "patchy" and would "like to see a more directed or cohesive policy": "I don't think there's an immediate person to person intervention about troubled kids or things like that" (Principal). However, it should be noted that personal/social development is quite high among pupils in these schools, a pattern which may reflect positive informal relations rather than the presence (or absence) of formal pastoral care structures:

> It's a good school with a nice atmosphere. [Staff] care about the pupils. (Teacher, school 5)

There is a very good relationship between staff and students, compared to other schools. (Teacher, school 5)

It's a kid-friendly school. (Teacher, school 6)

The majority of teachers in the six schools report that only a few pupils would talk to subject teachers about personal problems. There is little systematic variation between schools in these responses.

In summary, informal teacher-pupil relations may in some cases compensate for an absence of formal pastoral care provision. In the two more academically effective schools, management is quite critical of pastoral care provision but informal relations between management, teachers and pupils appear to be positive. It may be more difficult to rely on informal relations in larger schools or schools with more disadvantaged pupil intakes. In this respect, school 2 would appear to offer a model of good practice in developing student-centred provision coupled with pupil involvement in the school (see below).

11.12 PUPIL INVOLVEMENT IN THE SCHOOL

The extent and nature of formal pupil involvement vary between schools, although the relationship with pupil outcomes in the six schools is not clear-cut. Formal pupil involvement is particularly evident in two schools, school 2 and school 6, which use mentoring systems among pupils. School 2 provides a training programme in leadership skills for a number of fifth year pupils. Subsequently, three pupils take responsibility for each group of first year pupils and follow that group into second year. School 6 has a similar, but apparently somewhat less well developed, system. There are 30 pupils involved in their leadership programme. Their role is to "keep order", organise events and they play a role in "creating a certain sort of spirit within the school" (Principal). They "help with the running of the school and take care of first years" (Vice-principal). In addition, both schools have prefects elected by the pupils.

Pupil involvement, in a less formalised form, is also evident in school 4 which has a prefect system whereby elected prefects are involved with "induction and running programmes for the first years . . . and in dealing with problems that arise for fifth and sixth years" (Principal). In addition, there are regular assemblies for year and cycle groups, and a meeting with class tutors every morning. Unusually, pupils attend parent-teacher meetings in this school. School 1 also has a prefect system whereby prefects are elected by pupils but approved by the school. They organise activities for first years, and help out at parent-teacher meetings. They have some involvement in a representative capacity for pupils:

> They would have a meeting once a week with the year head of sixth year and some of the pastoral care people would be in there as well. And they would bring up issues that the students would want discussed and talked about. (Principal, school 1)

In addition, there are weekly year group assemblies and daily meetings with class tutors.

Two schools, one more academically effective and one less academically effective, have no formal pupil involvement within the school. In the more effective school, there are plans to introduce a system of pupil representation next year, and currently there is a committee of Transition Year pupils "to liaise with staff about the running of the Transition Year programme" (Principal, school 5). However, in the latter case, personal/social development was found to be highly positive among pupils, a pattern which may reflect more positive informal, rather than formal, relations within the school.

Information from the teachers' questionnaires indicates that teacher involvement in extra-curricular activities is highest in schools 5 and 1 (where over two-thirds of teachers have some involvement) and lowest in the less effective schools. However, low levels of involvement are also evident in the two girls' schools, a pattern which tends to reflect less involvement in sports. Satisfaction among teachers with the provision of extra-curricular activities is highest in school 1, the school with the highest level of pupil participation in such activities. Dissatisfaction is highest in schools 2 and 4.

11.13 PARENTAL INVOLVEMENT IN THE SCHOOL

The six schools show a similar pattern in relation to regular parent-teacher meetings, holding one per year for every year group. Attendance averages 90 per cent or more parents in schools 5, 6 and 1 (schools with comprehensive intakes), and around 80 per cent in schools 2, 3 and 4 (schools with more disadvantaged pupil intakes). However, a number of the schools hold additional information sessions for parents. In one of the more academically effective schools, information on junior cycle subject choice is sent home to parents and followed up by a parent-teacher meeting. There is no official information session for senior cycle parents, although information is sent home and there is a parent-teacher meeting for Transition Year parents: "and you would find parents coming in to us, and making special appointments with the career guidance teacher" (Principal, school 5). In school 4, there is a meeting regarding subject choice for parents at both junior cycle and senior cycle.

Three of the schools have home-school liaison (HSL) co-ordinators. In school 2, the role of the home-school liaison officer is:

> To visit homes; empowerment of parents through adult education courses; supporting parents in keeping their children at school; being a link between home and school, putting a human face on the school; networking with outside agencies: third-level institutions, health board [and] with primary schools. (HSL co-ordinator).

Initiatives include courses for parents with crèche facilities, "various courses such as computing, aerobics, flower arranging, personal development", and "informal meetings with parents of prospective first year students". According to the HSL co-ordinator, there have been "mixed results with the courses[6] [but] great success in starting with first year parents and bringing them through the school". The principal is very positive about this initiative:

> The school has become a more user-friendly place for them [parents] and they meet teachers just by the way, you know, kind of coming and going. (Principal, school 2)

> The introduction of home-school liaison has made the primary-secondary transition for first years better. It's a

---

[6] It should be noted that two parents interviewed were very positive about these courses, describing them as 'great', although acknowledging that attendance was variable.

> long process but it will improve parental input. (Teacher, school 2)

The role of the home-school liaison co-ordinator in school 3 is "to involve parents in the education of their children and keep them in school to the Leaving Cert" (HSL co-ordinator). Initiatives in the school have included a parents' room, along with parenting and other courses:

> Attendance has been poor. But there have been successful coffee mornings for first year parents where teachers introduce themselves and how the school works. The parents' room is successful. (HSL co-ordinator)

In school 4, the home-school liaison co-ordinator organises courses for parents "in response to what parents ask for" and has set up a parents' room in the school. However, their main role at the moment is out-reach work with parents, especially parents of first year pupils coming into the school:

> [The HSL co-ordinator] visits all of the families of the in-coming first years [and] would try and work out how the school could help them. (Principal, school 4)

> A minimum of 40 per cent of my time is spent on home visits; this sets the agenda. There are a lot of parents with bad vibes about school, low self-confidence. My role is that parents feel they can come in [to the school], see it as an integral part. . . . The target is the disadvantaged, families of at-risk kids. But there is a risk of labelling so I try to visit all of the families. Parents are usually early leavers themselves. (HSL co-ordinator, school 4)

Evaluating the success of the initiative, the HSL co-ordinator states:

> Going out is working fine; they [parents] are quite recep-tive. Getting them in is not so good but they are starting to see it [the school] as friendly.

In the two more effective schools, the principals take primary responsibility for dealing with parents.

All of the schools have a Parents' Association. These associa-tions have very diverse roles in the schools, ranging from fund-raising to involvement in policy development and planning. In school 5, the association plays an important information role "to keep us in touch with what's going on in school" (Parent), holding information evenings for parents, as well as running parenting courses. The Parents' Association in school 6 runs a book loan scheme for pupils; they also organise prize-giving for pupils and fund-raise for equipment, including computers. They organise mock orals and mock interviews for Leaving Cert pupils. They also have an information function, "we keep in touch between pupils and teaching staff" (Parent), holding information evenings and disseminating newsletters.

The main role of the Parents' Association in school 1, according to the principal, is fund-raising: "they nearly feel happiest doing that as well" (Principal). However, it does appear that they have tried to get involved in policy issues; they have been consulted on the school plan and themselves raised the issue of the school uniform:

> Years ago it [our role] was fund-raising, now we're more involved with running the school. (Parent, school 1)

They also "try to motivate other parents about new trends with guest speakers on drugs, discipline, exam motivation" (Vice-principal).

This tension between the "traditional" fund-raising role of parents and a move towards involvement in school planning is also evident, but from a different perspective, in school 2:

> Unfortunately they [the Parents' Association] see their main role as fund-raising whereas we'd be trying to get them into a more advisory role but it's difficult. (Principal, school 2)

The Parents' Association in school 3 has an "input into the ethos of the school, . . . curricular direction, fund-raising" (Principal):

> I would like to see the parents' association involved in a code of discipline. Their main function presently is fund-raising for books, equipment, a pitch, the book loan scheme. (HSL co-ordinator, school 3)

The role of the Parents' Association in school 4 is fund-raising, input into policy-making (especially on discipline), organising uniforms and lockers, financial support for "needy" students, and involvement in social events and outings.

Contact between the schools and the parents' associations is usually maintained through the principal, vice-principal and/or a staff representative.

A number of the schools reported difficulties in getting parents involved in events and meetings:

> There's apathy related to unemployment and it's very difficult to get [parents] involved. (Parent, school 6)

> The same faces are at everything. (Parent, school 1)

> It is hard to get parents to support you. (Parent, school 2)

> Parents are very wary of getting involved. (Parent, school 4)

> We don't get a chance to meet those [parents] whose children are not doing well. (Teacher, school 3)

Only school 5 appears to experience little of this difficulty:

> Parents are very helpful and keen to participate and be involved where necessary. (Vice-Principal, school 5)

In addition, in many cases the parents actively involved in the Parents' Associations may not be representative of the wider parent body within the school:

> I would have a very, very good working relationship with the people that are on the parents' committee, and they would work very hard on behalf of the school. There would be a small group of other parents who would work fairly hard on behalf of the school. But apart from that, we would have very little support for anything that we run. (Principal, school 4)

This issue has also been raised in relation to involvement in home-school liaison initiatives where parents with particular difficulties may be less likely to become involved (see Ryan, 1994).

School management tends to be positive about the role of the Parents' Association:

> We've a very good parent association and I work very closely with them. I attend all their meetings and keep very close to them. And we work very well together. (Principal, school 5)

> There's a terrific Parents' Association but it's few parents. (Principal, school 6)

Among teachers, perceptions of the Parents' Association are more positive in schools 6 and 3 than in other schools.

Teachers in the more academically effective schools are more likely to report higher expectations among parents for pupils in the school. Fairly high expectations in terms of going on to further education are also reported in school 1. This pattern mirrors parental expectations as reported by pupils themselves. Teachers in the more effective schools are also more likely to report that parents help their children with schoolwork. However, analyses of pupils' own responses show no significant differences between the more effective schools and others in the proportion of pupils reporting they receive help with their schoolwork from parents or siblings.

Two schools have distinctive characteristics in terms of parental involvement and staff attitudes to parents. Teachers in one of the more effective schools, school 5, have very positive views of parental support and involvement in the school. All of the teachers in school 5 report that "nearly all" parents think it is a good school while there is very little variation in responses among the other schools. Reported parental support for the school is again significantly higher in school 5 than in other schools. Perceived support is lower in the less effective schools and one of the average schools, school 2. Between-school differences in the pattern of parental attendance at meetings (as reported by teachers) are not statistically significant. However, reported attendance is somewhat better in schools 5, 6 and 1 and particularly bad in school 2. In addition, teachers in the more effective schools are less likely to complain about lack of parental support.

A number of these items were combined to give a scale of "reported parental support" (with an alpha value of 0.6). Parental support is found to be higher in the more effective schools, especially school 5. Values are lower in the less effective schools and school 2, all schools with more disadvantaged pupil intakes.

Teachers in school 2, while having less positive views of the level of parental support, express a very strong commitment to the involvement of parents in the school. All of the teachers in school 2 agree with the statement that "the school explains to parents what part they can play in their child's education". Teachers in school 2 are most likely to report that parents will receive support from the school if they have a particular problem. There is very little variation in responses among the other schools. The majority of teachers in the six schools report that they welcome meeting parents during the school day; responses are especially positive in schools 2 and 4. While there is no significant variation in the proportion of teachers who view parents as partners in the child's education, this view is more prevalent in school 2 than in other schools. A similar pattern is evident (i.e. within school 2) in relation to views on the organisation and importance of parent-teacher meetings. School 6 teachers also deem these meetings very important. Teachers in school 3 have a slightly more negative view of parent-teacher meetings than those in other schools. These nine items were combined to give a scale of "openness to parental contact" with an alpha value of 0.74. School differences are barely significant (p<.10) but school 2 has a higher degree of openness than other schools, despite a low reported level of parental involvement and attendance at meetings. This apparent contradiction may reflect the longer term nature of initiatives to encourage parental involvement in the school, whereby views are likely to change among the teaching staff and more involved parents before permeating to the parent body as a whole.

11.14 SCHOOL MANAGEMENT AND STAFFING

11.14.1 Division of labour in the school

A scale (with an alpha value of 0.65) measuring involvement in school decision-making, as reported by teachers, was derived. One of the more academically effective schools, school 5, scores highest in staff involvement. The majority of staff in school 5 report that they are at least somewhat involved in deciding the structure of classes, allocation of pupils to classes, the subjects offered, and subject choice; in addition, a substantial minority report some involvement in subject packaging. The two less effective schools have the lowest level of staff involvement in decision-making. However, school 6 which is "more academically effective" displays a similar pattern to the less effective schools. Among the "average" schools, school 2 shows somewhat greater staff involvement than school 1. In contrast to the other schools (except school 5), involvement in deciding the structure of, and allocation to, classes seems to be high in school 2.

The vast majority of teachers in the six schools report involvement in advising pupils on the level at which they take subjects; however, a substantial minority of those in the "less effective" schools report no such involvement.[7] The vast majority of teachers in all the schools report choosing textbooks for their own subjects; this pattern varies somewhat by school with high involvement in school 5 and lower involvement in school 3. Involvement in dealing with students' personal problems does not vary significantly by school. However, teacher involvement does appear to be somewhat higher in schools 5 and 2 and somewhat lower in school 6.

"Middle management" is organised somewhat differently in the six schools, using year heads, co-ordinators for particular groups (such as Transition Year or the Leaving Cert Applied programme), class tutors and/or subject department heads. Most, but not all, management positions are A- or B-posts. In addition, many positions which are very important in terms of management of the school (such as year head) are held by B-post holders (or those without a formal post) while some A-post holders are used for relatively unimportant tasks. Some dissatisfaction with the operation of the A- and B-post system has been expressed, in particular relating to the lack of suitability of particular staff for specific roles and the failure of the system to adapt to the changing needs of schools:

> I don't think they [the posts] are main-stream, there's nobody in charge of curriculum, there's nobody in charge of pastoral care . . . the A-posts . . . should have greater responsibility . . . it should be evident to everyone in the school what this person is in charge of and they should have a more administrative role. (Principal, school 6).

---

[7] This may relate to the high proportion of pupils in these schools taking ordinary levels only and/or the impact of streaming practices.

> They [the posts] are effective but they need to be over-hauled. I think that duties were assigned quite a long time ago and some would be no longer as they were and some would have become too large. (Vice-principal, school 4)

11.14.2 Teaching allocation

School management was questioned about the approach taken to allocating teachers to classes. First, there appears to be some effort taken in selecting particular teachers for the new second-level programmes:

> Certain people would be better at teaching weaker children and like it. (Principal, school 2)

The principal in school 1 reports that they are "very careful" about allocation for the remedial class, Transition Year and LCAP: "because it's a different method of teaching and a different approach". Second, two schools acknowledge that particular teachers are selected for Leaving Cert courses:

> There is a kind of unwritten approach that we would have our best teachers up-front teaching Leaving Cert honours subjects. (Principal, school 5)

> Some teachers can't be brought on to Leaving Cert. (Vice-principal, school 3)

Third, in a number of schools a "rotation" policy is adopted so that teachers have a chance to vary their workload and can also provide continuity for cohorts of students:

> There is no real system. They [teachers] try to carry the class all the way up. (Vice-principal, school 3)

> We try to give people a balance, a chance to teach different levels, different age-groups so their work is more interesting. (Vice-principal, school 4)

Analyses of teachers' current workloads, however, indicate little systematic variation between schools in the system of allocation of teachers. Only school 4 has a substantial proportion (18 per cent) of teachers specialising in teaching senior cycle groups.

11.14.3 Staff meetings

Formal staff meetings tend to be more frequent in the average schools, schools 1 and 2, with the majority of teachers reporting two or more meetings per term.[8] A significant minority of staff report two or more meetings per term in school 5. In contrast, meetings are less frequent in the "less effective" schools, once a term or less frequently. However, the majority of those in school 6 report that meetings are held once a term so management approaches may vary among "effective" schools. In a number of schools, "full" staff meetings are supplemented with year head meetings (school 5), sub-committee meetings (schools 5 and 6), subject meetings (school 4), a staff advisory council (school 4) and meetings of teaching teams (school 2).

The majority of staff in the more effective schools and in school 2 describe staff meetings as very important as does school management:

> People feel they're heard at staff meetings. (Teacher, school 5)

> [Staff meetings] tend to focus you. There is a small staff so there are good dynamics and an open relationship with the principal. (Teacher, school 2)

As might be expected, staff in schools with more frequent staff meetings tend to attribute more importance to them. In contrast, teachers and management in the "less effective" schools are less likely to describe meetings as very important and more than a quarter of teachers in these schools deem them "not important":

> Staff meetings don't achieve anything. Decisions aren't implemented. (Teacher, school 3)

> They [staff meetings] are useless as they currently tend to be briefings rather than meetings. The agenda is dictated from the top. (Teacher, school 4)

---

[8] It is interesting to note that there is variation within schools in the reported frequency of staff meetings. This may reflect differential awareness of the school's functioning on the part of teachers or variation in attendance at such meetings.

> People don't get enough chance to voice their opinions.
> (Teacher, school 4)

> It's a foregone conclusion. Decisions are made beforehand.
> If you go individually to the principal or vice-principal,
> they're very receptive but meetings don't work. (Teacher,
> school 4)

In spite of frequent meetings, school 1 has a similarly low "very important" rating but fewer totally disaffected staff:

> They [staff meetings] create an illusion of democracy. They
> benefit people who can voice their opinions. There are a
> few very vocal people who take over the drift of the meet-
> ing. Very often decisions are already made. They don't
> affect the decision-making process. (Teacher, school 1)

> They should be [important] but often they don't turn out
> like that. There is a big group. They're not as effective as
> they should be. (Teacher, school 1)

> I would favour breaking them up; with the year heads and
> the principal, it would be better to communicate. There is
> lowish attendance for the big meetings. Long meetings are
> not workable. (Teacher, school 1)

11.14.4 Development planning

Only two of the case-study schools have (or are in the process of developing) a written development plan and there is no clear relationship with "effectiveness" in pupil outcomes. At the time of the interviews, school 1 was in the process of drawing up a school development plan:

> A lot of it is putting in writing the policies and the existing
> structures that we have, writing it down so that if anyone
> comes in here, they can pick that up and know what we're
> about and what we're doing. It pins us down too to being
> specific about what we're doing and it also has provided
> the whole staff with an opportunity to know what other
> areas are doing. . . . And we also have to challenge
> ourselves on whether the policies we've had in the past are
> still viable or whether they need to be up-graded and

up-dated. [Is it done through staff meetings?] Yes. The
way we did it was we had a little core group and we wrote
what we thought was the existing plan or the existing
system. We wrote it up and what policies lie behind that
and then we had down long-term plan and short-term objectives. Then we broke up into groups and we asked if
this was a fair description. (Principal, school 1)

School 2 also has a written development plan:

We drew up targets for ourselves, I suppose four years ago
at this stage. And we're working out on those targets each
year and we do our report each year. That's the responsibility of the board of management and it's submitted to
the trustees of the school. It's working well because it
gives us a focus for planning and development throughout
the year. And also we know that we're going to have to
evaluate it at the end of the year so it keeps us more on
our toes, it's a good evaluation tool. (Principal, school 2)

There is no written development plan in school 5, although they
have drawn up a mission statement and the principal is eager to
draw up a school plan.

11.14.5 Management and staff relations

Teachers in two of the schools, schools 5 and 2, tend to report
more positive relationships with management and with their
colleagues. Teachers in these schools are more likely to report that
they are "always" listened to by the principal:

This is a good school . . . There are very good relations
among staff and a good relationship with management.
(Teacher, school 5)

Compared with other schools, staff are very much
respected by the principal. There's a very positive air in
the school. And teachers work hard in the school. There's a
good bond between the teachers. [It's] the best school I've
worked in. . . . The principal is very approachable and
always has time or will make time for you. (Teacher,
school 5)

> Everything is discussed before decisions are made. Staff are consulted. Decisions are taken jointly between the principal and teachers. (Teacher, school 5)

> There is a willingness to take on board new ideas in the school. . . . People are recognised, rewarded and heard. (Teacher, school 5)

> There is more teacher involvement in everyday decisions [than before]. (Teacher, school 2)

> There are a lot of discipline problems here but staff support each other a lot around these issues and ways to reward students. (Teacher, school 2)

The pattern in school 5 reflects the approach of the principal:

> What I'm trying to do is empower staff, I'm trying to be a chairman and be pretty democratic and cultivate the idea of collegiality amongst our staff here.

School 6, one of the more effective schools, shows a lower rate of satisfaction with management support than one of the less effective schools (school 4) but a higher rate than one of the average schools (school 1). This pattern is consistent with the variation among effective schools in management style apparent from the responses on involvement in decision-making (see above). Teachers in one of the less academically effective schools, school 3, are least likely to report that the principal "always" listens to them.

A fairly similar pattern is found in relation to reported support from management with more positive responses in schools 2 and 5. School 6 shows a similar pattern to school 4 with more negative responses in schools 1 and 3. However, these inter-school differences are not statistically significant.

There is no significant variation in the reported frequency of teachers' not being consulted about decisions, although those in the more effective schools have slightly more positive responses. There is no systematic variation in the proportion of teachers reporting that they get the resources to do their job, although responses are somewhat more positive in school 1 than in other schools.

Differences between schools in the reported incidence of talking to colleagues about teaching problems are not significant. However, responses in schools 2, 1 and 5 are somewhat more positive than those in other schools. Those in the less effective schools are more likely to report that they never or only sometimes talk to colleagues about problems. Similarly, there is very little variation in reported support from colleagues, although responses in school 3 are somewhat more negative than in other schools.

11.14.6 Job satisfaction among teachers

Teachers in schools 6 and 4 are slightly more likely to report that they always enjoy their work while teachers in school 3 are least likely to report this. A similar pattern is found when teachers are asked if they would prefer to be doing a different job with a clear difference between school 6 and other schools.

Between-school differences in the proportion of teachers who feel their abilities are recognised and rewarded are not statistically significant. However, those in schools 1 and 3 have less positive responses; in particular, two-fifths of the teachers in school 3 report that their abilities are never or only sometimes recognised.

Teachers in the more effective schools are more likely to report intrinsic job satisfaction, with the majority reporting that "nearly all" pupils are rewarding to work with. Responses are more negative in the other schools, especially school 2 where over a third of teachers reported that only a minority of pupils were rewarding to work with.

These items were combined into a scale of "job satisfaction". Job satisfaction is highest in the more effective schools, especially school 6, and lowest in school 3. The average and less effective schools overlap in terms of teacher satisfaction.

11.14.7 Staff development

The majority (83 per cent) of teachers interviewed in the six schools had taken part in in-service training during the previous three years. This pattern does not vary significantly between schools. However, schools do vary in the extent to which the school itself has been involved in providing training. In one of the "effective" schools (school 5), over half of the teachers mentioned courses provided in or by the school. The principal in school 5 has placed a strong emphasis on in-house staff development, having two staff days: one on drawing up a mission statement, another on pupil and teacher stress. School 6 has had a similar combination of in-house development and specific in-service courses (including management-related courses for class tutors and the Transition Year co-ordinator). However, staff in school 6 were less likely to mention school-based development when discussing their participation in training. School 2 also has in-house development during September which focuses on current issues.

Among teachers in the six schools, subject courses were the most frequently attended, three-fifths of all courses mentioned; this was highest in schools 6 and 1 and lowest in school 4. The next most frequently attended were courses for the new programmes, especially for the Leaving Cert Applied Programme. Over one-fifth of those in school 4 mentioned PLC or adult education courses, a pattern which is related to recent changes in the function of the school.

Broadly, staff are satisfied with the training courses they have attended; three-quarters of the teachers interviewed found these courses "very useful" or "useful". However, one person remarked that:

> The problem with in-service is it's too fragmented. Provision should be grouped to reflect the needs of particular children or schools. There's too much emphasis on subjects not style of teaching. (Vice-principal, school 4)

Training needs mentioned included "coping with change", pastoral care/pupil development, information technology and teaching methods (including mixed ability teaching):

> To develop teachers coming together and talking about teaching and learning and sharing on what works and doesn't work for them and being more open to more innovative ways of teaching in their own particular subject areas because of the demands, particularly in the new courses. (Principal, school 2)

11.14.8 Staff induction

The six schools vary in the approach taken to staff induction, although none of the schools have a very formalised approach to this issue. School 5 has a hand-book which is given to new teachers but the principal recognises the weaknesses in the current approach to staff induction:

> I should take them [new staff] aside for half a morning or
> a day and sit down with them and make it very clear to
> them what we expect with regard to teaching and disci-
> pline and ethos and so on. It's something I haven't done
> with teachers but in my view I should have done.

School 6 has no formal induction but recent appointments have
been part-time or substitute teachers "and that therefore means
that you put induction on a slow burner" (Principal).

In contrast, school 2 adopts a more formal approach to induction:

> What happens is with new staff the vice-principal would
> meet them on the first day when everybody isn't back and
> the children aren't back. And they'd go through all the
> nitty-gritty of school procedure and policy and how to deal
> with disruptive children and all that kind of stuff. And
> then we'd just check in and out with them in the course of
> the year, to make sure they're OK. (Principal)

In school 1, the principal states that:

> I'd say we might be a bit slack in that. Usually the
> younger teachers or whatever area they're going into . . .
> the group in that would take them on board. We'd give
> them the homework notebook and all the rules are in that.
> . . . But beyond that there's no structure.

There is no formal approach to induction in school 4 but appointments are generally made through part-time or substitute staff.

Teachers who had joined the staff in the previous three years
were questioned about the approach taken to integrating them
into the school. Only a very small minority mentioned any sort of
formal induction process and these teachers were in schools 2, 5
and 6:

> I was shown around the day I arrived and given a state-
> ment, the school aims and guideline for staff. (Teacher,
> school 5)

> I was brought in before the school term began. The rules
> and procedures were explained by the vice-principal. The
> staff were generally very helpful. (Teacher, school 2)

> It [induction] was quite good. I was brought in before term. The rules, discipline procedures, salaries and so on were explained. (Teacher, school 2)

New teachers in schools 1 and 4 were most likely to state that no specific approach was taken:

> There was very little done. It was up to myself to introduce myself to others. The staff were generally very helpful. (Teacher, school 4)

> I was left to my own devices. The staff were not particularly helpful. (Teacher, school 4)

> I was just thrown in at the deep end. (Teacher, school 1)

> I was left to my own devices. I got advice and help from the other [subject] teacher. (Teacher, school 1)

In the case of schools 5 and 3, informal induction by the principal was the most frequent response:

> The principal, vice-principal and every staff member made themselves known and offered advice. I never felt new or an outsider. Staff were very helpful; there was a helpful atmosphere. (Teacher, school 5)

> I was made most welcome by the principal and asked to take part in staff meetings and outings. (Teacher, school 5)

> The principal brought me around and introduced me. (Teacher, school 3)

> The principal showed me around but apart from this I had to deal with everything alone. (Teacher, school 3)

Those in schools 2 and 1 tended to mention informal induction by the other staff:

> There was no major input from the principal. I got help from other teachers. (Teacher, school 2)

On the formal level, there was very little. Informally, all
the staff were friendly. (Teacher, school 1)

11.15 SCHOOLS AND CHANGE

Schools must be considered as dynamic organisations with
on-going changes in the level and nature of their pupil intake,
their staffing, and the nature of the curriculum. Three of the six
case-study schools had experienced a change of school principal in
the three years since the survey of pupils. Levels of turnover
among other staff were low[9] and there was no significant difference between schools in the length of time teachers had been
employed. All of the schools had added or dropped subjects on the
curriculum and introduced new programmes for second-level or
post-second-level students (see above).

When questioned about changes in the schools, teachers most
frequently mentioned the appointment of a new principal and the
introduction of new programmes (such as LCAP, Transition Year,
Post-Leaving Cert courses). A significant minority (one-tenth) of
teachers in the more effective schools mentioned the introduction
of computers and/or new technology. A change in pupil intake was
a particularly important issue in school 2 and, to a lesser extent,
in school 5 while almost half the teachers in school 4 mentioned a
drop in pupil numbers. Teachers in school 2 mentioned improved
parent-teacher communication, a change in the discipline structures and a decline in the pupil work ethic. Increased workload
was mentioned by a significant minority of teachers in schools 6, 4
and 2.

When questioned about priorities for future development
within the school, an improvement of buildings/physical facilities
was mentioned by a number of teachers, especially in school 1 and
the more academically effective schools. To maintain or increase
pupil numbers was also of concern, especially in school 6 and, to a
lesser extent, schools 2 and 5. Staff in school 2 stressed the need
for more teachers and more emphasis on personal development:

---

[9] In contrast to some of the US research, there appears to be no clear
relationship between staff turnover and 'effectiveness', although this may
reflect the rather static nature of the labour market for teachers in Ireland.

> We need to continue the pastoral care approach in developing students as much as possible using existing resources [and] to respond to occurrences in society, such as drugs, and act accordingly. (Teacher, school 2)

An improvement in discipline was seen as a priority for a sizeable proportion of teachers in 1. Staff in the two more effective schools were more likely than others to mention "maintaining standards". In contrast, the development of PLCs were more likely to be mentioned by teachers in the less effective schools. The need for increased remedial provision was mentioned by almost one-fifth of teachers in schools 2 and 3. Improving pupil work ethic was mentioned by one-third of the teachers in school 1 and one-fifth of those in school 2:

> Finding a way to get [the pupils] to be more motivated and responsible for their work [is a priority]. . . . Developing that will be very important, especially for weaker students. (Teacher, school 2)

> Addressing the poor attitudes of pupils and attempting to get them more interested and involved in school [is a priority]. (Teacher, school 2)

> Encouraging a work ethic [is a priority]; pupils need greater encouragement to work harder. (Teacher, school 1)

Greater parental involvement was raised as an issue in school 2, in spite of higher levels of openness to parents than other schools. This may reflect higher expectations in relation to parental involvement among these teachers.

11.16 CONCLUSIONS

The case-studies of the six schools indicate some of the complex issues involved in school organisation and management. Schools vary along a number of dimensions, although these factors are not always clearly related to "effectiveness" in terms of pupil outcomes. It is clear, however, that improved academic and non-academic outcomes are closely associated with certain aspects of school practice.

More academically effective schools tend to be more flexible in relation to choice of subjects and subject levels, delaying a final decision in order to maximise the number of pupils taking higher level subjects. These schools tend to have a more orderly learning environment with lower levels of misbehaviour, apparently a consequence of a consistent approach to school discipline. In addition, teachers in more effective schools tend to have higher expectations of their pupils along with more positive perceptions of both pupils and parents. There tend to be more supportive relations among management and staff in the more effective schools, although management style may vary among effective schools (see Hallinger and Heck, 1998, for similar findings in other contexts). Many of these characteristics have been identified in effective schools in other national contexts (see Scheerens and Bosker, 1997, for comparable international findings). It should be noted that it may be more difficult to create this sort of school climate where schools are larger and/or have a more disadvantaged pupil intake. In this respect, it is interesting to consider the example of school 2 which differs from other schools with a disadvantaged pupil intake in terms of its strong emphasis on developing a flexible and responsive curriculum along with its positive efforts in integrating pupils and parents into the school.

Chapter 12

CONCLUSIONS AND POLICY RECOMMENDATIONS

This study has explored the impact of schooling factors on a range of pupil outcomes at Junior and Leaving Certificate level. The focus of the study is on identifying the key schooling processes which are associated with positive outcomes among pupils and can be used as a basis for developing models of good practice for all second-level schools. While previous studies have tended to focus on academic performance alone, the scope of this study is extended to include a consideration of other academic outcomes, such as absenteeism and pupil drop-out, and non-academic outcomes, such as self-image and stress levels. Such an approach allows us to explore the complex relationships between different aspects of pupil development over the schooling career. The study draws on both quantitative and qualitative data, setting the context using a national survey of second-level pupils and schools across Ireland and elaborating the general pattern through detailed case-studies of six schools. This chapter presents the main conclusions and policy implications of this research.

12.1 PUPIL BACKGROUND

A number of aspects of pupil background, in particular, gender, social class and age, have significant effects on educational outcomes. Girls now outperform boys in examinations, achieving higher grades overall and making greater progress relative to their initial ability. In addition, boys are much more likely than girls to report that they intend to leave school before the end of their second-level education. While there has been a recent decline in the proportion of young people leaving school before the Leaving Certificate, this small group is likely to become increasingly marginalised in terms of access to paid employment and further education/training.

New programmes (such as the Junior Certificate Schools Programme and the Leaving Certificate Applied Programme) have been recently developed at second-level in order to promote the retention of young people within full-time education. It is necessary to ensure that such provision is targeted on those pupils most at risk of early school-leaving and educational failure, in particular lower ability boys. Such targeting needs to take place at two levels. First, not all schools currently provide such programmes. Schools with particularly disadvantaged pupil intakes should be assisted in developing more flexible provision for their pupils. It is recognised, however, that the provision of additional programmes may be particularly difficult for smaller schools. In these cases, schools should be provided with support, for example through in-service training, in incorporating at-risk pupils into mainstream provision. Second, efforts should be made within schools to target new programmes towards pupils at risk of educational failure in order to reduce school drop-out and promote alternative channels of accreditation for lower ability pupils. It is hoped that these new second-level programmes will contribute to the development of more flexible progression routes within the system for lower ability pupils and that links into further education/training will be developed.

In spite of their higher performance, girls in second-level schools report higher stress levels, less sense of control over their lives and lower evaluations of their appearance than boys. There is a clear need for the development of personal/social development programmes which enhance self-image among girls and reduce stress levels among both sexes. In addition, such development programmes should address low self-esteem among lower ability pupils in order to integrate them fully into the educational process. Any formal programmes should be underpinned by a whole-school approach to promoting personal development and gender equity.

Pupils who are much older than average tend to underachieve in exams, especially at Junior Certificate level, and are more likely to intend to drop out of school early. These older pupils are likely to be made up of those who have been "kept back" a year or more in second-level or primary school. It does not appear, however, that this retention policy compensates for the learning difficulties experienced by this group. It would be preferable to focus on the provision of remedial assistance while keeping pupils with their age cohort.

Social class inequalities persist in academic achievement, absenteeism rates and drop-out rates. Furthermore, the social class context of the school has an additional effect on pupil outcomes, over and above a pupil's individual background. Working-class pupils in predominantly working-class schools tend to have lower exam grades, higher absenteeism, and higher drop-out rates than those in predominantly middle-class schools. This pattern highlights the need to provide extra resources and support to schools with intakes that are particularly disadvantaged, a process that has been initiated with the Breaking the Cycle programme. In addition to providing resources, such interventions should focus on the promotion of other aspects of effective schooling, including the development of a positive school climate, promoting higher expectations for and among pupils, greater parental and pupil involvement in the school, and positive relations between pupils, parents and teachers.

12.2 ABSENTEEISM AND DROP-OUT

The research indicates a strong relationship between absenteeism and school drop-out. Those pupils who have poor attendance records are more likely to report that they intend to leave school after the Junior Certificate exam. It is recommended that pupils with high absenteeism levels should be targeted for school-level intervention, thus reducing potential drop-out. Measures should include home-school liaison and the promotion of positive pupil-teacher relations within the school in the context of co-ordinated support from local and national services, such as the school attendance service and psychological services.

Schools should be encouraged to adopt formal programmes (such as the Junior Certificate Schools Programme) which are aimed at reducing early drop-out. At the same time, schools should be encouraged to develop more informal and flexible initiatives at the school level which will better integrate potential leavers into the school.

12.3 SCHOOL EFFECTIVENESS

There has been much debate, especially in the British context, about the need to develop performance indicators for individual schools. To this end, "league tables" have been compiled which indicate the relative ranking of schools in Britain in terms of their exam performance. This study indicates that such an approach would be inappropriate in the Irish context. Knowing a particular school's average performance in "raw" terms tells us little about the difference the school actually makes to its pupils. An above average ranking in these terms may merely reflect a selective pupil intake. In contrast, another school may have lower exam results but its pupils may have made considerable academic progress relative to their initial ability levels.

Much of the difference between second-level schools in pupil outcomes (both academic and non-academic) is, in fact, due to differences in the intake of pupils to the school. However, schools do differ in terms of their impact on pupil outcomes so in the Irish context "schools matter". The nature of school effectiveness is highly complex, however, and must be regarded as outcome- and group-specific. Analyses indicate that schools are rarely consistently "effective" (or "ineffective") across the whole range of pupil outcomes, both academic and non-academic. Schools with improved academic progress among pupils do not necessarily have equally positive effects on pupil development. However, there is some consistency among dimensions of academic effectiveness. Pupil absenteeism and drop-out rates tend to be lower in schools which enhance academic progress among pupils. In addition, schools which enhance a particular aspect of pupil development, such as academic self-image, tend to have positive effects on other aspects, such as sense of control.

There is some evidence of differential effectiveness in second-level schools, that is, schools may not be equally effective for different groups of pupils, in particular those of different ability levels. Some schools are found to maximise the difference in exam performance between higher and lower ability pupils while other schools minimise this initial difference. Analyses indicate that schools vary more in the academic performance of lower ability pupils, in other words, schools make more of a difference for this group. This pattern requires that we pay attention not only to the "average" performance of the school but also to (in)equality of outcomes within the school.

In general, the research findings highlight the need for greater specificity in discussions of school effectiveness. Before specifying whether a school is "effective", we need to clarify both the outcome in question (e.g. academic performance, pupil drop-out, self-image) and the particular group or groups with which we are concerned (e.g. different ability levels, girls or boys). Schools are rarely exceptionally "effective" or "ineffective" across the whole range of pupil outcomes, a pattern which makes the identification of

broadly effective schools more difficult. In addition, the imprecision involved in ranking schools even in relation to one particular
outcome, such as academic performance, means that a "league
table" approach is inappropriate. A much more valuable exercise
involves shifting attention away from the evaluation of individual
schools towards focusing on the schooling factors associated with
particular dimensions of academic and personal/social development among pupils. The following sections discuss some of the
most significant school characteristics identified by this research
in order to highlight good practice in the second-level sector.

12.4 CLASS ORGANISATION

The system of class allocation used has important consequences
for a number of pupil outcomes. Streaming tends to have negative
consequences for pupils allocated to bottom classes without
securing any overall advantages for those allocated to the top
classes. At Junior Certificate level, the average pupil in highly
streamed schools tends to do somewhat worse in exams than those
in schools with mixed ability base classes. At both Junior and
Leaving Certificate level, being in a bottom class in a streamed
school results in significant underperformance in exams, even
controlling for initial ability. Furthermore, those in bottom classes
are more likely to intend to drop out of school early.

In the case-study schools, many managers and teachers have
expressed concern about the difficulty of using mixed ability
teaching methods, especially in the context of existing curricular
demands for higher level courses. There appears to be a need to
provide information to schools and teacher training institutions on
the potential consequences for pupils of using ability-based differentiation. In-service training should be available to support
schools who wish to use mixed ability teaching and/or setting
within their school.

Remedial provision, usually based on withdrawal from ordinary class, is available to pupils in all of the case-study schools. A
number of issues have been raised within these schools but
further research is necessary in order to explore the nature of
remedial provision across the whole second-level sector. First, the
extent of remedial provision in the case-study schools, in terms of
staffing and teaching hours, does not appear to reflect the scale of
literacy and numeracy difficulties in these schools. Second, provision tends to be targeted on pupils in the junior cycle, especially

those in their first year. While this approach is likely to facilitate the transition of pupils into second-level education, requirements for remedial assistance among older cohorts are likely to be increasingly evident as more and more pupils stay on to the end of the senior cycle. Third, existing provision tends to be targeted on English. While literacy skills undoubtedly underpin progress within all subject areas, other areas such as Maths could benefit from remedial assistance.

12.5 CURRICULUM AND SUBJECT CHOICE

A more open approach to subject choice has positive consequences for pupils. Pupils tend to do somewhat better in their exams when subject choice occurs later in the junior or senior cycles, allowing pupils to explore the range of subjects which suit their needs and abilities. Conversely, pupils tend to report higher stress levels where they feel the school is not responsive to their needs and where they have not been able to choose the subjects they wanted.

The way in which subjects are made available to pupils within a school needs to be given more attention in policy terms (see *Charting Our Education Future*, p.46). In particular, support should be provided to schools in relation to later timing of subject choice through, for example, a system where pupils are allowed to "sample" different subjects before making a final choice. Many teachers have expressed concern about the difficulty of providing a broad range of subjects in the context of declining pupil (and therefore staff) numbers. Initiatives, such as co-operation among schools in a local area in the provision of certain subjects, should be encouraged in order to facilitate pupil choice. However, it may be necessary to go further than this by recognising that curricular diversity is resource-intensive for schools and taking account of this through the funding mechanism. In the context of projected decreases in pupil numbers at second-level, the promotion of curricular diversity as a means of maximising later educational and career choices on the part of pupils should not be ignored.

A detailed consideration of the processes shaping the provision, allocation and choice of subjects is outside the parameters of the current study. However, schools in the sample are found to differ significantly in the way they make choices available to pupils of different ability levels. Attention should be paid to providing the widest possible choice even to those in "bottom" classes. In addition, subjects should be packaged in such a way as to facilitate non-traditional subject choices for girls and boys.

The case-studies of schools indicate that the more academically effective schools facilitate as many pupils as possible in taking higher level subjects. This is achieved by delaying the final choice about the take-up of higher rather than ordinary level courses. Schools should be encouraged to develop a more open approach to access to higher level courses, through the development of mixed ability and setting systems, rather than assigning pupils to a particular level on the basis of their class allocation.

12.6 PUPIL INVOLVEMENT

The issue of pupil involvement within a school has received relatively little attention in national discussions concerning school policy. However, the study indicates that pupils tend to do better academically and are less likely to drop out when they are more integrated into the school, for example, through pupil councils/prefect systems or informally through extra-curricular activities. Two of the case-study schools have well-developed mentoring systems, whereby older pupils take an active role in integrating younger pupils into the second-level school. Such an approach could provide a model for good practice in other schools and is likely to be particularly important in providing positive role models for pupils who may previously have had negative experiences of the schooling process.

Pupil involvement should be considered as a feature of management and in-service training within schools. Schools should be encouraged to develop structures, such as pupil councils, to facilitate communication between teachers and pupils (see *Charting Our Education Future*, p.163). Formal pupil involvement should be underpinned by positive informal relations between the staff and pupils. In this respect, schools should be given practical support (through additional resources, for example) to expand the range of extra-curricular activities on offer to pupils. At present, schools with more disadvantaged pupil intakes are likely to be at a disadvantage in securing additional "voluntary" funding from parents for such activities.

12.7 PARENTAL INVOLVEMENT

The limited information available on parental involvement in the sampled schools indicates a positive association between the extent of such involvement and pupil outcomes. More detailed information on the case-study schools indicates that schools vary in the extent of parental involvement, the existence of formal structures or initiatives to encourage such involvement, and the role of parents' associations in the school. Parental involvement would appear to be lower in schools based in urban and/or more disadvantaged areas. Formal initiatives, such as the home-school liaison scheme, designed to encourage such involvement have met with some success (see Ryan, 1994) but must be seen in terms of a much longer term process of developing school-community links. Such initiatives are likely to be much more successful where an openness to parental involvement permeates the whole school rather than responsibility being limited to one person (e.g., the principal or home-school co-ordinator).

The role of formal parents' associations ranges from fund-raising to involvement in policy development within the school. Parental participation in events tends to be higher for practical activities (such as fund-raising and book loans schemes) and information sessions than for more policy-oriented tasks. In addition, representatives of parents' associations report difficulties in involving other parents in such activities.

Schools should be given support to involve parents in the formal and informal life of the school. Such support could take place through the existing home-school liaison scheme, through in-service training for specific teachers or through co-ordination with other local groups (e.g., local area partnerships, adult education providers etc.). While such activities may justifiably be targeted on schools in disadvantaged areas, there is a need to extend such an approach across the second-level sector, at least in part because not all pupils from disadvantaged backgrounds attend schools in disadvantaged areas.

12.8 DISCIPLINARY CLIMATE

The disciplinary climate of the school has a significant impact on academic outcomes among pupils. Pupils tend to do better academically in schools which are "strict but fair" and where there is less disruption of learning time through pupil misbehaviour. Disciplinary climate also has an effect on pupil drop-out with pupils less likely to drop out of schools which are characterised as strict. The important elements appear to be the creation of an orderly learning environment for pupils along with the clear and consistent application and enforcement of school rules, both in general terms and in the specific case of homework policy.

The disciplinary climate of the school is likely to play an important part in the dynamic of school improvement (or disimprovement). Declining standards of pupil behaviour may result in more negative pupil-teacher interaction which in turn may lead to lower expectations and less consistency in the application of sanctions. The development of clear codes of behaviour for pupils within a school is necessary in order to break this cycle. Department of Education circulars have already disseminated information on suggested practice in relation to school discipline (Circular M33/91). However, many teachers stress the need for outside support for schools in developing and enforcing a disciplinary code. It is recommended that the dissemination of information on good practice should be supplemented with in-service training for school management and staff in this area.

12.9 TEACHER-PUPIL INTERACTION

The research indicates a strong relationship between the quality of teacher-pupil interaction and academic and development outcomes among pupils. Pupils tend to do better in their exams where they receive positive feedback from teachers concerning their school work. Conversely, pupils do worse academically and are more likely to drop out of schools when they experience poor relations with teachers. In addition, pupils tend to respond to the expectations of teachers within the school, making greater academic progress where teachers expect them to stay on in full-time education. High (but realistic) expectations on the part of management and teachers have been seen as a crucial dimension of school effectiveness (see, for example, Sammons *et al.*, 1997). The creation of a positive academic climate is underpinned by positive relations between teachers and pupils and among staff (see below). While it is difficult to intervene directly in this area, the importance of feedback to pupils and the development of a whole-school approach to assessment and feedback should be given attention in initial and continuing teacher training.

Positive pupil-teacher interaction is also associated with enhanced developmental outcomes, including lower stress levels, more positive self-image and greater sense of control among pupils. Unless formal programmes to enhance pastoral care and pupil development within the school are underpinned by emphasising positive pupil-teacher interaction at the informal level, they are likely to be of limited utility. Teacher training and in-service courses should emphasise the importance of informal interaction and the need for regular support and feedback to pupils. At present, time-tabling pressures create difficulties for schools in providing formal pupil development programmes. However, an emphasis on personal/social development is likely to have positive effects for pupils in personal and academic terms and such provision should be supported in terms of resources and staff development. Such programmes are likely to be particularly important where schools have a high intake of pupils from disadvantaged backgrounds.

Pupils who experience bullying in school tend to have much higher stress levels, lower body image and less sense of control over their lives. Schools should be encouraged to develop and implement clear policies and effective practice on bullying and to provide support for those pupils who have experienced bullying. This process has been initiated through a Department circular (Circular M42/93) on the topic and should be reinforced through in-service training and back-up support for schools.

12.10 SCHOOL MANAGEMENT

Less academically effective schools appear to be characterised by less staff involvement in decision-making in the school, less emphasis on formal staff meetings, less positive relations between management and staff, and less supportive relations among colleagues. There is some variation among more academically effective and "average" schools in the management style adopted. However, one of the case-study schools shows the clear positive impact of a strong emphasis on collegiality and staff participation in decision-making on academic and non-academic pupil outcomes.

The development of positive and supportive relations among management and staff may be more difficult to achieve in a larger school. As the demands on schools increase in scale and complexity, greater attention should be paid to the development of middle management structures. Support should be given to schools in developing formal structures for communication, decision-making and planning, and in developing management positions within the school. In-service training should be provided to facilitate the development of these management skills among those in middle and senior managerial positions within the school.

12.11 STAFF DEVELOPMENT

A high proportion of teachers have taken part in in-service training in recent years. However, much of this training has been driven by the requirements of new programmes and revised curricula. Consequently, less time has been available for teachers to take courses in other areas, such as teaching methods (e.g., mixed ability teaching) and management skills. The more academically effective schools have had a greater emphasis on whole school development with in-house programmes specifically tailored to address the needs of the particular school. The complexity of the tasks faced by schools requires that greater emphasis should be given to the development of the whole school rather than to discrete subject areas or programmes. Support should be provided to schools in developing such a whole school approach to development. Measures required would include management training and in-career development for teachers.

None of the case-study schools have had a highly formalised approach to staff induction, although a greater emphasis on integrating new teachers into the school is evident in the more academically effective schools. A recent report (Swan and Leydon, 1997) has stressed the need for more structured induction for newly qualified teachers. However, more structured induction is likely to be useful for all newly appointed teachers. More innovative approaches, such as staff mentoring, could be used as a way of integrating new teachers into the day-to-day life of the school. As schools vary in their organisation and approach, attention to teacher induction is likely to lead to greater consistency within the school in relation to discipline, homework policy and expectations of pupils.

12.12 SCHOOL DEVELOPMENT

Only two of the case-study schools have (or are in the process of developing) a written development plan and there is no clear relationship with "effectiveness" in pupil outcomes. However, less academically effective schools tend to be characterised by less consultation between management and staff and lower levels of parental involvement in school development (see above). The significant influence of several dimensions of school organisation and process on academic and non-academic outcomes among pupils indicates the importance of adopting a whole-school approach to development and planning. Such an approach requires support in terms of management and teacher training and in terms of information.

Analyses have indicated the redundancy of crude "league table" approaches to school evaluation. Ranking schools in terms of their aggregate exam scores tells us little about the processes at work in a particular school or about how to enhance pupil outcomes within that context. However, information on pupil outcomes can be a useful tool for schools in their own planning and development. Schools could, for example, monitor their own attendance and drop-out rates as a basis for introducing new programmes or adapting existing provision. However, information collected at the school level is likely to be of limited utility without comparable information on the national context. An investigation of the possibility of providing value added analyses to schools would be worthwhile. Such an approach would require information on pupil ability at the point of entry and ideally some additional information (through surveys, for example) on pupil background (see Croxford and Robertson, 1996). It would be an absolute requirement that any such information should be confidential with schools provided with their own results along with the national pattern. This information could be used by the school itself in setting targets for improvement and in monitoring the introduction of new programmes or teaching methods.

In conclusion, it should be recognised that schools are dynamic organisations, continually adapting to changes in pupil intake, staffing levels and curricular provision. The research indicates that second-level schools are confronted with an increasingly diverse set of goals and tasks in an attempt to enhance academic and social development among their pupils. The purpose of research on school effectiveness should be to provide information and models of good practice to schools in order to enhance their capacity to bring about school improvement.

BIBLIOGRAPHY

Aitkin, M. and N. Longford (1986). "Statistical Modelling Issues in School Effectiveness Studies", *Journal of the Royal Statistical Society A*, Vol. 149, No. 1, pp.1-43.

Birnbaum, I. (1994). "The Statistics of Value Added", in N. Hill (ed.), *Value Added Analysis: Current Practice in Local Education Authorities*. Slough: National Foundation for Educational Research.

Breen, R. (1986). *Subject Availability and Student Performance in the Senior Cycle of Irish Post-Primary Schools*, General Research Series, No. 129, Dublin: The Economic and Social Research Institute.

Breen, R., D.F. Hannan and R. O'Leary (1995). "Returns to Education: Taking Account of Employers' Perceptions and Use of Educational Credentials", *European Sociological Review*, Vol. 11, No. 1, pp.59-73.

Brookover, W., C. Beady, P. Flood, J. Schweitzer, J. Wisenbaker (1979). *School Social Systems and Student Achievement: Schools Can Make a Difference*. New York: Praeger.

Brophy, J. and T.L. Good (1986). "Teacher Behaviour and Student Achievement", in M.C. Wittrock (ed.), *Handbook of Research on Training*, New York: Macmillan.

Bryk, A.S., V.E. Lee, P.B. Holland (1993). *Catholic Schools and the Common Good*. Cambridge, Mass.: Harvard University Press.

Bryk, A.S. and S.W. Raudenbush (1988). "Toward a More Appropriate Conceptualization of Research on School Effects: a Three-level Hierarchical Linear Model", *American Journal of Education*, Vol. 97, pp.65-108.

Bryk, A.S. and Y.M. Thum (1989). "The Effects of High School Organization on Dropping out: an Exploratory Investigation", *American Educational Research Journal*, Vol. 26, No. 3, pp.353-383.

Casey, B. and D. Smith (1995). *Truancy and Youth Transitions*, London: Department for Education and Employment.

Cheng, Y. (1995). *Staying On in Full-Time Education After 16: Do Schools Make a Difference?* London: Department for Education and Employment.

Coleman, J.S., E. Campbell, C. Hobson, J. McPartland, A. Mood, F. Weinfeld, and York, R. (1966). *Equality of Educational Opportunity Report*, Washington, DC: Government Printing Office.

Coleman, J.S., T. Hoffer, and S. Kilgore, (1982). *High School Achievement*, New York: Basic Books.

Creemers, B.P.M. and G.J. Reezigt (1996). "School Level Conditions Affecting the Effectiveness of Instruction", *School Effectiveness and School Improvement*, Vol. 7, No. 3, pp.197-228.

Creemers, B.P.M. and J. Scheerens (1994). "Developments in the Educational Effectiveness Research Programme", in R.J. Bosker, B.P.M. Creemers and J. Scheerens (eds.), *Conceptual and Methodological Advances in Educational Effectiveness Research*, Oxford: Elsevier.

Croxford, L. and M. Cowie (1996). *The Effectiveness of Grampian Secondary Schools*, Edinburgh: Centre for Educational Sociology.

Croxford, L. and B. Robertson (1996). *A Collaborative Approach to Indicators of Quality in Grampian Secondary Schools*, Paper to the School Effectiveness and School Improvement Seminar, CES.

Department of Education (1991). *A Suggested Code of Behaviour and Discipline for Post-Primary Schools*, Circular M33/91.

Department of Education (1993). *Guidelines on Countering Bullying Behaviour in Primary and Post-Primary Schools.* Circular M42/93.

Department of Education (1995). *Charting Our Education Future: White Paper on Education*, Dublin: Stationery Office.

Department of Education (1996). *Key Education Statistics 1984/85-1994/95.* Dublin: Stationery Office.

Drudy, S. and M. Ní Chatháin (1996). *The Reflective Teacher: Insights from Observation of Gender Differences in Classroom Interaction at Second Level*, Paper to the Gender Equality for 2000 and Beyond Conference, Dublin.

Dustmann, C., N. Rajab and A. van Soest, (1996). *Part-time Work, School Success and School Leaving*, London: UCL Discussion Paper.

Earley, P., B. Fidler and J. Ouston, (eds.) (1996). *Improvement Through Inspection? Complementary Approaches to School Development*, London: David Fulton.

Eckstein, Z. and K.I. Wolpin, (1998). *Youth Employment and Academic Performance in High School*, London: Centre for Economic Policy Research, Discussion Paper No. 1861.

Firestone, W.A. (1991). "Introduction", in J.R. Bliss, W.A. Firestone and C.E. Richards (eds.), *Rethinking Effective Schools: Research and Practice*, New Jersey: Prentice Hall.

Gamoran, A. and M. Nystrand (1994). "Tracking, Instruction and Achievement", in R.J. Bosker, B.P.M. Creemers and J. Scheerens (eds.), *Conceptual and Methodological Advances in Educational Effectiveness Research*, Oxford: Elsevier.

Goldstein, H. (1995). *Multilevel Statistical Models. Second Edition*, London: Edward Arnold.

Goldstein, H. (1997). "Methods in School Effectiveness Research", *School Effectiveness and School Improvement*, Vol. 8, No. 4, pp.369-395.

Goldstein, H. and M.J.R. Healy (1995). "The Graphical Presentation of a Collection of Means", *Journal of the Royal Statistical Society*, Series A, Vol. 158, No. 1, pp.175-177.

Goldstein, H., Rasbash, J., Yang, M., Woodhouse, G., Pan, H., Nuttall, D. and Thomas, S. (1993). "A Multilevel Analysis of School Examination Results", *Oxford Review of Education*, Vol. 19, No. 4, pp.425-433.

Goldstein, H. and D.J. Spiegelhalter (1996). "League Tables and their Limitations: Statistical Issues in Comparisons of Institutional Performance", *Journal of the Royal Statistical Society*, Series A, Vol. 159, No. 3, pp.385-443.

Gray, J. (1995). "The Quality of Schooling: Frameworks for Judgement", in J. Gray and B. Wilcox, (eds.), *"Good School, Bad School": Evaluating Performance and Encouraging Improvement*, Milton Keynes: Open University Press.

Gray, J., D. Jesson, H. Goldstein, K. Hedger, and J. Rasbash (1995). "A Multi-level Analysis of School Improvement: Changes in Schools' Performance Over Time", *School Effectiveness and School Improvement*, Vol. 6, No. 2, pp.97-114.

230 *Do Schools Differ?*

Gray, J., D. Jesson and N. Sime (1990). "Estimating Differences in the Examination Performances of Secondary Schools in Six LEAs: a Multi-level Approach to School Effectiveness", *Oxford Review of Education*, Vol. 16, No. 2, pp.137-158.

Hallinger, P. and R.H. Heck (1998). "Exploring the Principal's Contribution to School Effectiveness: 1980-1995", *School Effectiveness and School Improvement*, Vol. 9, No. 2, pp.157-191.

Hannan, D.F., M. Boyle (1987). *Schooling Decisions: The Origins and Consequences of Selection and Streaming in Irish Post-Primary Schools*. General Research Series No. 136, Dublin: The Economic and Social Research Institute.

Hannan, D.F., R. Breen, B. Murray, D. Watson, N. Hardiman, K. O'Higgins (1983). *Schooling and Sex Roles*, General Research Series no. 113, Dublin: The Economic and Social Research Institute.

Hannan, D.F., S. Ó Riain (1993). *Pathways to Adulthood in Ireland*. General Research Series no. 161, Dublin: The Economic and Social Research Institute.

Hannan, D.F., D. Raffe, E. Smyth (1996). *Cross-National Research on School to Work Transitions: An Analytical Framework*. Background paper to the OECD.

Hannan, D.F., E. Smyth, J. McCullagh, R. O'Leary, D. McMahon (1996). *Coeducation and Gender Equality. Exam Performance, Stress and Personal Development*, Dublin: Oak Tree Press/The Economic and Social Research Institute.

Hanushek, E.A. (1986). "The Economics of Schooling: Production and Efficiency in Public Schools", *Journal of Economic Literature*, Vol. 24, pp.1141-1147.

Hill, N. (ed.) (1994). *Value Added Analysis: Current Practice in Local Education Authorities*, Slough: National Foundation for Educational Research.

Jencks, C., M. Smith, M. Bane, D. Cohen, H. Gintis, B. Heynes and S. Michelson (1972). *Inequality: A Reassessment of the Effects of Family and Schooling in America*, New York: Basic Books.

Jesson, D. and J. Gray (1991). "Slants on Slopes: Using Multi-level Models to Investigate Differential School Effectiveness and its Impact on Pupils' Examination Results", *School Effectiveness and School Improvement*, Vol. 2, No. 3, pp.230-247.

Jones, K. (1991). *Multi-Level Models for Geographical Research*, Norwich: University of East Anglia.

Jones, K. (1992). "Using Multilevel Models for Survey Analysis", in Westlake, A., R. Banks, C. Payne and T. Orchard, (eds.), *Survey and Statistical Computing*, Amsterdam: North-Holland.

Kendall, L. (1995). "Contextualization of School Examination Results 1992", *Educational Research*, Vol. 37, No. 2, pp.123-139.

Knuver, A.W.M. and H.P. Brandsma (1989). "Pupils' Sense of Well-being and Classroom Educational Factors", in B. Creemers, T. Peters, D. Reynolds (eds.), *School Effectiveness and School Improvement*, Amsterdam: Swets and Zeitlinger.

Kreft, I. and J. De Leeuw, (1998). *Introducing Multilevel Modeling*, London: Sage.

Lee, V.E. and A.S. Bryk, (1989). "A Multilevel Model of the Social Distribution of High School Achievement", *Sociology of Education*, Vol. 62, pp.172-192.

Lee, V.E. and J.B. Smith, (1995). "Effects of High School Restructuring and Size on Early Gains in Achievement and Engagement", *Sociology of Education*, Vol. 68, pp.214-270.

Lee, V.E., A.S. Bryk and J.B Smith (1993). "The Organization of Effective Secondary Schools", *Review of Research in Education*, Vol. 19, pp.171-267.

Leithwood, K.A., S.B. Lawton, and J. Bradley Cousins (1989). "The Relationship between Selected Characteristics of Effective Secondary Schools and Student Outcomes", in B. Creemers, T. Peters, D. Reynolds (eds.), *School Effectiveness and School Improvement*, Amsterdam: Swets and Zeitlinger.

Loeb, S. and J. Bound, (1996). "The Effect of Measured School Inputs on Academic Achievement: Evidence from the 1920s, 1930s and 1940s Birth Cohorts", *Review of Economics and Statistics*, Vol. LXXVIII, No. 4, pp.653-664.

Madaus, G., T. Kellaghan and E. Rakow (1975). *A Study of the Sensitivity of Measures of School Effectiveness*, Dublin: Educational Research Centre.

Mandeville, G.K. and L.W. Anderson, (1987). "The Stability of School Effectiveness Indices Across Grade Levels and Subject Areas", *Journal of Educational Measurement*, Vol. 24, No. 3, pp.203-216.

McCoy, S., B.J. Whelan, (1996). *The Economic Status of School Leavers 1993-1995*, Dublin: ESRI/ Dept. of Education/ Dept. of Enterprise and Employment,

McNeal, R.B. (1997). "Are Students being Pulled Out of High School? The Effect of Adolescent Employment on Dropping Out", *Sociology of Education*, Vol. 70, No. 3, pp.206-220.

Mortimore, P., P. Sammons, L. Stoll, D. Lewis and R. Ecob (1988). *School Matters: The Junior Years*, London: Open Books.

National Commission on Education. (1996). *Success Against the Odds: Effective Schools in Disadvantaged Areas*, London: Routledge.

Nuttall, D.L., H. Goldstein, R. Prosser, and J. Rasbash (1989). "Differential School Effectiveness", *International Journal of Educational Research*, Vol. 13, No. 7, pp.769-776.

Ouston, J., E. Earley, and B. Fidler (eds.) (1996). *OFSTED Inspections: The Early Experience*, London: David Fulton.

Paterson, L. (1991). "Socio-economic Status and Educational Attainment: a Multi-dimensional and Multi-level study", *Evaluation and Research in Education*, Vol. 5, No. 3, pp.97-121.

Preece, P. (1989). "Pitfalls in Research on School and Teacher Effectiveness", *Research Papers in Education*, Vol. 4, No. 3, pp.47-69.

Purkey, S.C. and M.S. Smith (1983). "Effective Schools: a Review", *Elementary School Journal*, Vol. 83, No. 4, pp.427-452.

Rasbash, J. and G. Woodhouse (1995). *MLn Command Reference*, London: Institute of Education.

Reynolds, D. (1995). "The Effective School: an Inaugural Lecture", *Evaluation and Research In Education*, Vol. 6, No. 2, pp.57-73.

Rowe, K.J. and P.W. Hill (1994). *Multi-level Modelling in School Effectiveness Research: How Many Levels?* Paper to the International Congress for School Effectiveness and Improvement, Melbourne.

Rutter, M., B. Maughan, P. Mortimore, and J. Ouston (1979). *Fifteen Thousand Hours: Secondary Schools and their Effects on Children*, London: Open Books.

Ryan, S. (1994). *Home-School-Community Liaison Scheme: Final Evaluation Report*, Dublin: Educational Research Centre.

Sammons, P., J. Hillman, P. Mortimore (1995). *Key Characteristics of Effective Schools: A Review of School Effectiveness Research*, London: Institute of Education.

Sammons, P., D. Nuttall, and P. Cuttance (1993). "Differential School Effectiveness: Results from a Reanalysis of the Inner London Education Authority's Junior School Project data", *British Educational Research Journal*, Vol. 19, pp.381-405.

Sammons, P., S. Thomas, and P. Mortimore (1997). *Forging Links: Effective Schools and Effective Departments*, London: Paul Chapman.

Sammons, P., S. Thomas, P. Mortimore, C. Owen, H. Pennell, J. Hillman (1994). *Assessing School Effectiveness: Developing Measures to put School Performance in Context*, London: Institute of Education.

Scheerens, J. (1992). *Effective Schooling: Research, Theory and Practice*, London: Cassell.

Scheerens, J. and R.J. Bosker (1997). *The Foundations of Educational Effectiveness*, Oxford: Pergamon Press.

Slater, R.O. and C. Teddlie (1992). "Toward a Theory of School Effectiveness and Leadership", *School Effectiveness and School Improvement*, Vol. 3, No. 4, pp.242-257.

Smith, D.J. and S. Tomlinson (1989). *The School Effect: A Study of Multi-Racial Comprehensives*, London: Policy Studies Institute.

Smyth, E., D.F. Hannan (1995). *1985/86 School Leavers: A Follow-up Study in 1992*, The Economic and Social Research Institute Working Paper no. 65.

Sorenson, A. and M. Hallinan (1984). "A Reconceptualization of School Effects", *Sociology of Education*, Vol. 50, pp.273-289.

Sui-Chu, E.H. and J.D. Willms (1996). "Effects of Parental Involvement on Eighth-grade Achievement", *Sociology of Education*, Vol. 69, pp. 126-141.

Swan, D. and M. Leydon (eds.) (1997). *Teacher Induction*. Dublin: Standing Committee of Teacher Unions and University Education.

Teddlie, C. and S. Stringfield (1993). *Schools Make A Difference: Lessons Learned from a 10-Year Study of School Effects*, New York: Teachers College Press.

Thomas, S. and P. Mortimore (1996). "Comparison of Value-added Models for Secondary-school Effectiveness", *Research Papers in Education*, Vol. 11, No. 1, pp.5-33.

Thomas, S., P. Sammons, P. Mortimore and R. Smees, (1997). "Differential Secondary School Effectiveness: Comparing the Performance of Different Pupil Groups", *British Educational Research Journal*, Vol. 23, No. 4, pp.451-469.

Willms, J.D. (1985). "The Balance Thesis: Contextual Effects of Ability on Pupils' O-grade examination results", *Oxford Review of Education*, Vol. 11, No. 1, pp.33-41.

Wilson, B.L. and T.B. Corcoran (1988). *Successful Secondary Schools*, London: Falmer Press.

Woodhouse, G. (1995). *A Guide to MLn for New Users*, London: Multilevel Models Project, Institute of Education.

Woodhouse, G. and H. Goldstein (1988). "Educational Performance Indicators and LEA League Tables", *Oxford Review of Education*, Vol. 14, No. 3, pp.301-320.

Woodhouse, G. and H. Goldstein (1996). "The Statistical Analysis of Institution-based Data", in H. Goldstein and T. Lewis (eds.) *Assessment: Problems, Developments and Statistical Issues*, London: John Wiley.